SCOTTISH CERTIFICATE OF EDUCATION

Credit and General GERMAN

The Scottish Certificate of Education Examination Papers
are reprinted by special permission of
THE SCOTTISH QUALIFICATIONS AUTHORITY

ISBN 0 7169 9271 x
© Robert Gibson & Sons, Glasgow, Ltd., 1998

*The publishers have wherever possible acknowledged the source of copyright material. They regret any
inadvertent omission and will be pleased to make the necessary acknowledgement in future printings.*

ROBERT GIBSON · Publisher
17 Fitzroy Place, Glasgow, G3 7SF.

CONTENTS

SCOTTISH
CERTIFICATE OF
EDUCATION
1995

TUESDAY, 23 MAY
10.10 AM – 10.55 AM

GERMAN
STANDARD GRADE
General Level
Reading

When you are told to do so, open your paper and write your answers **in English** in the spaces provided.

You may use a German dictionary.

Before leaving the examination room you must give this book to the invigilator. If you do not, you may lose all the marks for this paper.

Your German pen friend has sent you some magazines to read.

1. This article is about the Highland Games in Scotland.

Sport auf Schottisch

Marks

Match the words to the pictures. Write the correct letter in each box.

	Letter
Eine ganze besondere Attraktion ist das Baumstammwerfen. Ein 5,90 Meter langer Stamm muß möglichst weit geworfen werden.	
Gespannt verfolgen jedes Jahr Tausende von Zuschauern die Wettkämpfe.	
Beim Gewichthochwurf müssen 25 Kilogramm über die Latte geworfen werden.	
In Schottentracht bekleidet wird beim Dudelsackspielen traditionell getanzt.	
Dudelsackkapellen spielen bei allen Highland Games.	

(4)

2. You read an article about holidays on a farm.

Ferien auf
dem Bauernhof

Urlaub auf dem Land ist vor allem für Stadtkinder unheimlich interessant. Die Unterkunft ist meistens nicht sehr teuer, und wenn ihr bei einer netten Familie wohnt, dürft ihr richtig teilnehmen am Leben auf dem Bauernhof. Ihr könnt dort lernen, eine Kuh zu melken oder Hühner und Schweine zu füttern.

Praktisch dabei ist, das man zwar früh aufstehen und helfen kann, aber nicht muß.

What are the good points about holidays on a farm?

Tick (✓) **three** things which are mentioned.

	Tick (✓)
It's not too expensive.	
You can help with the harvest.	
You can feed the animals.	
You can drive a tractor.	
You don't need to help if you don't want to.	

(3)

3. This article is about what German people do in their free time.

Marks

90%:	Musik hören
83%:	Fernsehen
78%:	Zeitungen lesen
74%:	Gut essen gehen
68%:	Parties feiern
68%:	Zeitschriften lesen
57%:	Radfahren
56%:	Autofahren
55%:	Bücher lesen
53%:	Wandern
48%:	Kochen, Backen
42%:	Sport treiben

Freizeit-Vergnügen

Von je 100 Bundesbürger beschäftigen sich in ihrer Freizeit am liebsten mit:

Die Deutschen sind in ihrer Freizeit nicht besonders aktiv. Am liebsten hören sie schöne Musik. Dann kommt auf dem zweiten Platz Fernsehen. Auf dem letzten Platz dagegen steht Sport und nur 53% der Befragten gehen gern wandern. 74% der Leute gehen gern aus und dann vor allem, um gut zu essen.

Complete the table below.

90%:	....
83%:	Watching television
78%:	Reading newspapers
74%:	....
68%:	Going to parties
68%:	Reading magazines
57%:	Cycling
56%:	Motoring
55%:	Reading books
53%:	....
48%:	Cooking, baking
42%:	....

(4)

4. In the magazine a young girl called Melanie is complaining about the area where she lives.

Kein Platz für Kinder?

Melanie ist sauer: „In unserer Straße wohnen viele Kinder. Aber hier fahren die Autos immer viel zu schnell durch. Hauptsache, die Erwachsenen kommen schnell zur Arbeit. Es stinkt auch immer nach Abgasen. Etwas weiter weg von unserer Wohnung gibt es einen Spielplatz. Aber es wird zur Zeit in einen Parkplatz für Autos umgebaut."

Melanie hat in ihrer Klasse von ihrem Problem erzählt. Die Klasse hat vor, einen Brief an die Zeitung zu schreiben.

Marks

(*a*) What is she complaining about? Write **three** things. **(3)**

_____

_____

_____

(*b*) What is the class going to do about it? **(1)**

_____

7

5. Three young people are in a school class in Germany with pupils from various countries.

They did not like being in the school at first.

> Am Anfang hatte ich große Angst vor den Schulpausen, weil keiner mit mir sprechen wollte.
>
> **Dennis (Jugoslawe)**

> Am Anfang hat es mich sehr gestört, daß mehr ausländische Kinder als deutsche Kinder in der Klasse waren. Jetzt ist Rania aus Syrien meine Freundin.
>
> **Steffi (Deutsche)**

> Zuerst ging ich immer traurig nach Hause. Die anderen Schüler haben mich immer ausgelacht, weil ich die Sprache nicht konnte. Aber mit der Zeit ging es viel besser. Jetzt bin ich mit vielen deutschen Schülern befreundet.
>
> **Tom (Amerikaner)**

Marks

	Why did they not like being in the school at first? Write **one** thing for each person.
Dennis	
Steffi	
Tom	

(3)

6. In this article three young people write about what is on their mind at the moment.

Meine größte Sorge ist die Schule. Ich weiß nicht, ob ich die Oberstufe schaffen werde. Falls nicht, weiß ich im Moment überhaupt nicht, was ich dann machen soll. Ich möchte gern in einer Bank arbeiten, aber es ist sehr schwer, eine Stelle zu bekommen.

Philip, 14

Vor Drogis habe ich Angst. Letzte Woche abends ist einer auf mich zugekommen, und hat mir meinen Geldbeutel gestohlen. Seitdem traue ich mich abends nicht mehr allein auf die Straße.

Joschka, 16

Meine Mutter heiratet morgen. Dann sind wir endlich nicht mehr allein zu Hause, meine Mutter und ich. Das wird ein komisches Gefühl sein, aber trotzdem freue ich mich darauf. Mit Muttis Freund komme ich sehr gut aus.

Laura, 13

Marks

Complete the grid below.

Name	What they have on their mind	Why? Write **two** things for each person.
Philip	School	
Joschka	Drug addicts	
Laura	Home life	

(6)

7. Another article is about two young people who collect things.

Sandra collects wrappers from paper hankies.

Bei einer Klassenfahrt in die Schweiz habe ich mir zwei Päckchen Papiertaschentücher gekauft. Weil mir die bunte Verpackung so gut gefallen hat, begann ich vor zwei Jahren, solche Packungen zu sammeln. Inzwischen besitze ich schon 153 Stück, die aus fast allen Ländern Europas stammen. Immer wenn ich in fremde Städte oder ins Ausland komme, gehe ich durch Supermärkte oder Drogerien und suche nach neuen Packungen. Vielleicht komme ich einmal ins Guinness Buch der Rekorde . . .?

Sandra Wildner

Christian collects glass ornaments.

Bei einem Ausflug mit dem Kindergarten entdeckte ich an einem Andenkenstand eine Schneekugel, in der ein Fisch zwischen Korallen und Meerespflanzen schwimmt. Da ich sie unbedingt wollte, schenkte sie mir meine Mutter. Seitdem kaufe ich mir von meinem Taschengeld ab und zu eine Schneekugel, und auch von Freunden und Bekannten aus anderen Ländern bekomme ich welche. Ich hätte sehr gern eine Schneekugel aus Japan.

Christian Haack

Complete the grid below.

	Sandra	**Christian**
How did they start their collections? Write **one** thing for each person.		
How do they add to their collections? Write **two** things for each person.		
What is each collector hoping for?		

(8)

Total (32)

[END OF QUESTION PAPER]

SCOTTISH
CERTIFICATE OF
EDUCATION
1996

TUESDAY, 28 MAY
10.10 AM – 10.55 AM

GERMAN
STANDARD GRADE
General Level
Reading

When you are told to do so, open your paper and write your answers **in English** in the spaces provided.

You may use a German dictionary.

Before leaving the examination room you must give this book to the invigilator. If you do not, you may lose all the marks for this paper.

Marks

A group from your German exchange school came to Scotland recently. They left some newspapers and magazines for you to read.

1. You look at some adverts for houses and flats.

A
Stadtmitte—möbliertes Zimmer mit Küche. Ab sofort zu vermieten.

B
Dachgeschoßwohnung am Stadtrand. Bushaltestelle direkt vor der Tür.

C
Exklusives Einfamilienhaus (mit Doppelgarage), auf 11 Wohnräume verteilt, in sehr angenehmer, ruhiger Lage am Stadtrand.

D
Große Ein-Familien-Villa, circa 200 Meter zur Stadtmitte.

E
Bezugsfertig circa Dezember 1996. 3-Zimmer Villa mit Garage.

Which would suit the following people? Write the correct letter in each box. **(4)**

	Letter
A family who want a large house near the town centre.	
A couple with a car looking for a brand new house.	
A student looking for a room in the town centre.	
A family who want a large house in a quiet area.	

2. You see this cartoon.

„Ich konnte bei dem Nebel die Schule nicht finden!"

The boy hasn't been to school today. What excuse is he giving his mum? **(1)**

3. This article is about a very special hotel.

> ## Kleinstes Hotel der Welt steht jetzt in Bremen
>
> Etwas Außergewöhnliches hat die Stadt Bremen anzubieten. In Bremen steht das kleinste Hotel der Welt.
>
> Das Hotel hat Platz für maximal zwei Personen. Es hat keine Rezeption, aber es hat im Erdgeschoß ein kleines Speisezimmer, im ersten Stock einen kleinen Fernsehraum und im zweiten Stock das Schlafzimmer.

(*a*) What is special about the hotel?	**(1)**
(*b*) How many floors does it have? Write a number in the box.	**(1)**
(*c*) How many rooms does it have? Write a number in the box.	**(1)**

4. You look at some of the headlines in a newspaper.

A
> **Pilotin mit zwölf Jahren**

B
> **Dreijähriges Kind verschwunden**

C
> **Junger Dieb gefangen**

D
> **Bei 110 auf der Autobahn**

E
> **Rettungswagen verunglückt**

Match the headlines to the articles. Write the correct letter in each box.   **(4)**

Letter

Der 14jährige Andreas Kracht hat aus einem Wagen Autoradio, Pocketkamera sowie eine Taschenlampe gestohlen.

Ein Krankenwagen blockierte gestern abend die Hauptstraße.   Er ist mit einem Mercedes zusammengestoßen.

Dr. Lars Müller überholte auf der Autobahn Köln-Bonn, als er plötzlich das Bewußtsein verlor.

Seit zwei Wochen suchen die Polizeibehörden Aachen die kleine Marliese Orff (3).

Die Amerikanerin ist die jüngste Fliegerin, die je den Atlantik überquert hat.

5. In this magazine article five young people say what problems they have at home.

Ich darf meine Kleider nicht selber wählen. Das ärgert mich sehr.

Maria, 17

Alle meine Freunde fahren zusammen auf Urlaub. Ich darf nicht mit.

Frank, 16

Zu Hause muß ich den Tisch decken, mein Zimmer aufräumen, aber meine Schwester macht überhaupt nichts.

Walter, 14

Wenn ich auf eine Party gehe, holt mein Vater mich immer ab.

Anke, 16

Am Wochenende muß ich pünktlich um 11 Uhr zu Hause sein.

Anette, 15

What problems do they have?

Fill in the grid. **(5)**

	Problem
Maria	
Frank	
Walter	
Anke	
Anette	

6. You read an article about a fox.

Der Fuchs

Der Fuchs ist ein bißchen kleiner als ein Wolf.
Seine Augen haben die gleiche Form wie die einer Katze.
Er ist rot und hat einen weißen Bauch.
Sein buschiger Schwanz ist fast so lang wie sein Körper!
In der Nacht sieht er viel besser als am Tag.
Vor allem aber hört er sehr gut.
Der Fuchs verbringt seine Tage damit, Felder und Wälder zu durchstreifen,
Und an den Flußufern entlangzulaufen.

What does the article tell us about the fox?   **(5)**

His eyes (Write **two** things)	
His tail	
His ears	
How he spends his days	

Marks

7. You read a review of some new books in a magazine.

Henk Barnard **Mutti, wo bist du?**	Michelle Magorian **Der Junge zieht ein**
A	**B**
Allan F. Jones **Sie liebt mich, sie liebt mich nicht . . .**	Elisabeth Petersen **Mein Haus hat Räder**
C	**D**

Match the words to the correct book. Write the correct letter in each box.　　(3)

	Letter
In der Türkei versteckt sich der 11jährige Aydin in einem holländischen Lastwagen, um zu seiner Mutter zu kommen, die in Rotterdam lebt.	
Nicky und Donna, beide 15, gehen schon eine Weile miteinander. Sie freuen sich auf die Sommerferien. Dann kommt alles ganz anders.	
Ein Junge findet bei einem einsamen alten Mann ein neues Zuhause.	
Für den 15jährigen Sinti Schawo bedeutet das Leben im Wohnwagen Probleme.	

8. Four young people give their opinions about school uniform. Melanie and Stefan are against school uniform.

> Eine Uniform tragen? Das kann ich mir nicht vorstellen. Jeden Tag das gleiche anziehen, das ist doch langweilig. Das würde mir gar nicht gefallen.
>
> Melanie

> Die Schuluniformen, die ich bisher gesehen habe, mag ich nicht. Ich möchte nicht Kleider anziehen, die mir vielleicht überhaupt nicht stehen.
>
> Stefan

(*a*) Why are they against school uniform? Give **one** reason for each person. **(2)**

Melanie	
Stefan	

Bettina and Katharina are in favour of school uniform.

> Ich bin ein Jahr in Australien zur Schule gegangen und habe dort eine Uniform getragen. Das finde ich gut. Man weiß immer, was man tragen soll.
>
> Bettina

> Ich möchte eine Uniform tragen. Wenn alle gleich aussehen wie in englischen Schulen, finde ich das gut. Es gibt keine Konkurrenz unter Schülern. Man braucht sich nicht jeden Tag modisch anzuziehen.
>
> Katharina

(*b*) Why are Bettina and Katharina in favour of school uniform? Give **one** reason for each person. **(2)**

Bettina	
Katharina	

Marks

9. You receive a letter from your pen friend. She writes about terrible weather they have had in Germany.

Holzhausen, den 1. 3. 1996

Hallo!

Mir geht es gut. Und Dir?
War es bei Euch in Scotland auch so schlimm mit dem Gewitter? Ich konnte heute nacht kaum schlafen, da ich immer Angst hatte, mein Fenster breche aus den Angeln. Es hat so gekracht. Mitten in der Nacht fiel der Strom aus und ich mußte mich im Dunkeln bis zu einer Taschenlampe tasten. Am Morgen kam die Nachricht im Radio, daß alle Kinder in Bayern schulfrei hätten.

(a) What was she afraid might happen during the storm? **(1)**

_____

(b) What happened in the middle of the night? **(1)**

_____

(c) What did she hear on the radio? **(1)**

_____

Total (32)

[END OF QUESTION PAPER]

SCOTTISH
CERTIFICATE OF
EDUCATION
1996

TUESDAY, 28 MAY
2.20 PM – 2.45 PM
(APPROX)

GERMAN
STANDARD GRADE
General Level
Listening Transcript

Instructions to reader(s):

For each item, read the English **once,** then read the German **twice**, with an interval of 7 seconds between the two readings. On completion of the second reading, pause for the length of time indicated in brackets after each item, to allow the candidates to write their answers.

Where special arrangements have been agreed in advance by the Board to allow the reading of the material, those sections marked **(f)** should be read by a female speaker and those marked **(m)** by a male: those sections marked **(t)** should be read by the teacher.

(t) You have just arrived at Munich airport to spend some time with your pen friend, Erich.

Question number one.

Your pen friend explains how you will travel to his house.

Which two forms of transport will you use? Tick **two** of the boxes.

How long will the journey take?

(m) **Mein Vater ist immer noch bei seiner Arbeit. Wir müssen also mit dem Bus zum Hauptbahnhof fahren und dann weiter mit der U-Bahn zur Maillingerstraße. Wir werden in einer Stunde zu Hause sein.**

(30 seconds)

(t) Question number two.

You arrive at Erich's house. His mother greets you.

What does Erich's mother suggest you might want to do? Tick **two** of the boxes.

(f) **Willkommen in München! Du bist bestimmt müde. Möchtest du dich vielleicht ein bißchen im Bett ausruhen? Dann kannst du später deine Familie anrufen, um ihnen zu sagen, daß du gut angekommen bist.**

(30 seconds)

(t) Question number three.

Erich suggests you visit the Olympic village the next day.

What does Erich's mother say you can do at the Olympic village? Tick **two** of the boxes.

(m) **—Morgen können wir zum Olympiazentrum fahren, wenn du Lust hast.**

(f) **—Ja, Erich. Dort kann man viel unternehmen, nicht wahr? Ihr könnt vielleicht schwimmen gehen und am Nachmittag den Fernsehturm besuchen.**

(30 seconds)

24

(t) Question number four.

On your way to the Olympic village the next day, Erich points out some of the sights.

What does he tell you about the BMW museum? Write **two** things.

(m) **Hier rechts ist das BMW Museum. Dort kann man sowohl viele alte Autos sehen, als auch die neuesten Modelle. Vor allem kann man dort auch sehr schnelle und teure Autos bewundern. Nur fahren darf man sie nicht!**

(30 seconds)

(t) Question number five.

After visiting the Olympic village, you go to a snack bar for lunch. Erich has decided what he wants to eat.

What does Erich want to eat? Write **two** things.

What question does he ask you?

(m) **Ich nehme eine Bratwurst ohne Senf und eine Portion Pommes mit Mayo. Möchtest du auch eine Bratwurst oder lieber etwas anderes?**

(30 seconds)

(t) Question number six.

During lunch Erich talks about a film he would like to see.

Why does he particularly want to see this film? Write **three** things.

(m) **Im Kinocenter läuft ein Film, den ich sehr gerne sehen würde. Mein Bruder hat diesen Film neulich gesehen und hat ihn toll gefunden. Mein Lieblingsschauspieler, Robin Williams, spielt darin die Hauptrolle. Der Film ist sehr spannend und auch total lustig.**

(30 seconds)

(t) Question number seven.

Later in the evening you discuss plans for the following day. Erich is at school in the morning and he suggests that **you** spend the morning looking for souvenirs to take home.

Which souvenirs does Erich recommend? Tick **two** of the boxes.

(m) **In der Kaufingerstrasse gibt es eine große Auswahl von Geschäften. Da kannst du bestimmt viele Andenken von München kaufen. Viele Touristen kaufen Bierkrüge, Lederhosen und Filzhüte. An deiner Stelle würde ich ein Poster von den Sehenswürdigkeiten Münchens und eine weißblaue Fahne kaufen.**

(30 seconds)

(t) Question number eight.

Erich suggests how you could spend the afternoon.

What does he suggest you do? Write **two** things.

m) **Zuerst können wir einen Spaziergang durch zwei schöne Gärten machen, den Hofgarten und den Englischen Garten. Dann werden wir die Universität besichtigen.**

(30 seconds)

(t) Question number nine.

During the evening Erich talks about some of the lessons he has at school the following day.

Why does he not like Maths? Write **two** things.

(m) Mathe mag ich überhaupt nicht. Wenn die Lehrerin mir eine Frage stellt, weiß ich nie die Antwort. Oft bekommen wir auch zu wenig Zeit, die Aufgaben fertigzurechnen.

(30 seconds)

(t) Question number ten.

Erich tells you what he hopes to study at university and talks about his plans for the rest of the summer.

What plans does Erich have for the summer? Write **two** things.

(m) Nächstes Jahr hoffe ich Biologie hier in München zu studieren. Aber mein Vater ist zur Zeit arbeitslos. Ich muß also einen Ferienjob finden, um Geld für das Studium zu verdienen. Wenn dann noch Zeit bleibt, werde ich vielleicht einen Freund in Hamburg besuchen fahren.

(30 seconds)

(t) Question number eleven.

Erich tells you about what he did last summer.

What kind of work did he do in America last summer?

What comments does he make about what he did? Write **two** things.

(m) Letztes Jahr war ich in Amerika. Ich habe dort vier Wochen in einer Sommerschule für Jugendliche gearbeitet. Obwohl ich nicht besonders gut bezahlt wurde, hatte ich die Chance, meine Sprache zu verbessern und Amerikaner kennenzulernen.

(30 seconds)

(t) End of test.

You now have 5 minutes to look over your answers.

[END OF TRANSCRIPT]

Your school has an exchange link with a German school. You are helping to prepare a newsletter in German to send to the German school.

1. You write a short description of your school's Headteacher.

   You could say, for example, what his/her name is, what age he/she is (roughly!), what he/she is like.

   Try to write at least **three** sentences. Write in **German**.

2. Write a little about your school.

   You could say, for example, where the school is, when it begins, how long a lesson lasts, what subjects pupils take.

   Try to write at least **three** sentences. Write in **German**.

3. Tell the German pupils what there is to see and do in your area.

For example: Man kann den Naturpark besuchen.

Try to write at least **three** sentences. Write in **German**.

4. Write a little about what you did during a recent visit to Germany.

You could mention, for example, a place you went to, how you got there, what you thought of it.

Try to write at least **three** sentences. Write in **German**.

5. The German pupils will come to Scotland next summer. There is a café not far from your school where everyone meets. Use the plan below to write directions from your school to the café.

Write in **German**.

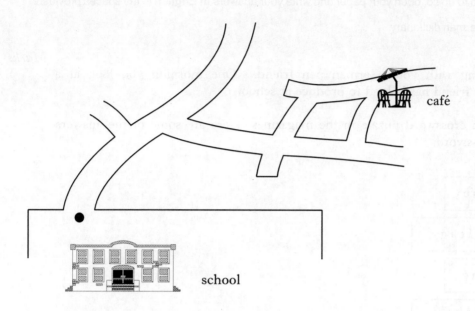

café

school

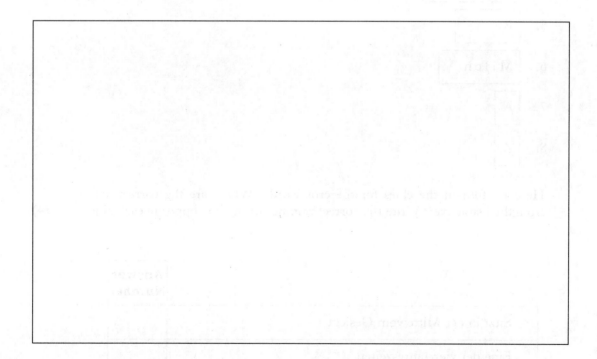

[END OF QUESTION PAPER]

SCOTTISH
CERTIFICATE OF
EDUCATION
1997

WEDNESDAY, 28 MAY
11.05 AM – 11.50 AM

GERMAN
STANDARD GRADE
General Level
Reading

When you are told to do so, open your paper and write your answers **in English** in the spaces provided.

You may use a German dictionary.

Marks

You are staying with your German pen friend. One morning you look at a magazine your friend has helped to produce at school.

1. There is a crossword puzzle in the magazine. Here are some of the answers to the crossword.

    1. | N a s e |
    2. | F r e i t a g |
    3. | K i n o |
    4. | F r ü h l i n g |
    5. | B e i n |
    6. | M i l c h |
    7. | A |
    8. | Z |

    Here are four of the clues for the crossword. Which are the correct answers from the list above? Write the correct number in the box opposite each clue. **(4)**

	Answer Number
Sitzt in der Mitte vom Gesicht	1
Eine der vier Jahreszeiten	4
Hier kann man Filme sehen	3
Letzter Buchstabe im Alphabet	8

Marks

2. There is an article by a girl called Michaela. She writes about the advantages of having a computer at home.

Ich habe vor einem Jahr einen Computer zum Geburtstag bekommen. Mit dem Computer zu schreiben ist einfach. Meine Hausaufgaben schreibe ich jetzt alle mit dem Computer. Wenn ich Fehler mache, gehe ich einfach zurück und übertippe den Fehler.

Tick (✓) **two** of the boxes to show whether the following statements are **true** or **false**.

(2)

	True	False
Michaela bought the computer with her pocket money.		✓
She does all her homework on the computer.	✓	

Marks

3. You see this advertisement for a local hotel.

Verbringen Sie einen schönen Urlaub im

Landhaus Haake

Genießen Sie die ruhige Lage auf dem Land.

Viele schöne Wanderwege, teils durch den Wald, in der Nähe.

Winterangebot bis 30. April 1998

3 Wochen wohnen
2 Wochen bezahlen!

Wir freuen uns auf Ihren Besuch

(a) Why would people want to go to this hotel? Write **two** things. **(2)**

To Enjoy the quiet peaceful countryside location
There are lots of beautiful, walker ranges + trails
through the woods nearby

(b) What special offer is the hotel making for the winter? **(1)**

Stay for 3 weeks for price of 2 weeks

Marks

4. A girl called Margarete talks about a part-time job she has at McDonald's.

Ich arbeite schon seit zwei Jahren bei McDonalds. Ich bin einfach hingegangen und habe gefragt, ob 'was frei ist, und sie haben gesagt, okay, fang bei uns an.

Wir sind ein gutes Team. Vier an der Kasse, vier in der Küche. Seit sechs Monaten bin ich jetzt Schichtführerin. Das heißt, ich bediene nicht mehr die Gäste. Ich passe nur auf, daß alles gut läuft.

(*a*) How did Margarete manage to get the job at McDonald's? **(1)**

_____

(*b*) How has her job changed in the last six months? Write **two** things. **(2)**

_____

_____

5. This article gives some tips for a healthy life-style.

Zum Fit- und Gesundbleiben gehört gesundes Essen. Das heißt:

- Zuviel Alkohol soll man vermeiden. Er hat viele Kalorien und kann zu schweren Krankheiten führen.

- Zuviel Salz und salzige Nahrungsmittel sind ungesund.

- Nicht viel Zucker essen. Süßigkeiten machen dick. Frisches Obst oder Obstsaft ist besser.

- Nicht rauchen! Rauchen schadet dem ganzen Körper; es macht die Haut grau und führt oft zu Lungenkrebs!

According to the article, why should we avoid the following things? Give **one** reason for each. **(4)**

Too much alcohol	
Too much salt	
Too much sugar	
Smoking	

Marks

6. These young people were asked: do you like living in Germany or would you prefer to live in a different country?

Ceyda

Ich würde lieber in der Türkei leben. Da ist es wärmer, und da wohnen mein Opa und meine Oma. Deutschland gefällt mir, aber nicht so gut wie die Türkei.

Kurt

Ich würde lieber in Italien wohnen. Da kann man im Winter gut Ski fahren. Es gibt überall in den Bergen Sesselbahnen. Es macht Spaß, damit hochzufahren.

(*a*) Ceyda and Kurt would prefer to live in another country. Why? **(4)**

	Would prefer to live in . . .	Why? Give **two** reasons for each.
Ceyda	Turkey	1. 2.
Kurt	Italy	1. 2.

Sascha

Es gefällt mir gut hier in Deutschland. Man hat hier gute Arbeitsmöglichkeiten, und ich habe nette Freunde in der Schule.

(*b*)   Sascha likes living in Germany. Why?   **(2)**

	Likes living in . . .	Why? Give **two** reasons.
Sascha	Germany	1. 2.

7. Three young people talk about what they do to protect the environment.

Thomas

- Ich tue, was ich kann. Auch meine Familie. Wenn wir durch den Wald wandern, nehmen wir Tüten mit und sammeln den Abfall auf.

- Wir bringen auch unsere alten Kleider zu einer Sammelstelle.

Ecki

- Ich fahre so wenig wie möglich Auto. Meiner Meinung nach liegt das Hauptproblem bei den Autoabgasen.

- Ich werfe auch kein Papier auf die Straße.

Susanne

- Bei uns zu Hause trennen wir den Hausmüll—Aluminium, Altpapier und Plastik.

- Für die Schule kaufe ich nur Hefte aus Altpapier.

What do they do for the environment? Write **two** things for each person.

(6)

Thomas	
Ecki	
Susanne	

Marks

8. Here are your pen friend's answers to a questionnaire in the magazine. The questionnaire is about how energetic or how lazy people are. (Your friend's answers are the ones marked with a cross.)

Bist du energisch oder faul?

1. **Dein Freund hat dich für den Abend eingeladen. Er wohnt fünf Kilometer von dir entfernt. Wie kommst du zu ihm?**

(a) Deine Mutter fährt dich mit dem Auto hin und holt dich abends wieder ab. ☒

(b) Die ganze Strecke ist gut beleuchtet. Du fährst also mit dem Fahrrad zu deinem Freund. ☐

2. **Es regnet, und du mußt zur Schule. Meistens gehst du den Weg zu Fuß. Was machst du heute?**

(a) Du sagst deiner Mutter, daß du krank bist. Du gehst heute nicht in die Schule. ☐

(b) Du ziehst eine Regenjacke an und gehst trotz des schlechten Wetters zu Fuß. ☒

What is the first situation described in the questionnaire?	
What would your pen friend do in this situation?	

What is the second situation described in the questionnaire?	
What would your pen friend do in this situation?	

(4)

[END OF QUESTION PAPER]   **Total (32)**

SCOTTISH
CERTIFICATE OF
EDUCATION
1997

WEDNESDAY, 28 MAY
1.00 PM – 1.25 PM
(APPROX)

GERMAN
STANDARD GRADE
General Level
Listening Transcript

Instructions to reader(s):

For each item, read the English **once,** then read the German **twice,** with an interval of 7 seconds between the two readings. On completion of the second reading, pause for the length of time indicated in brackets after each item, to allow the candidates to write their answers.

Where special arrangements have been agreed in advance to allow the reading of the material, those sections marked **(f)** should be read by a female speaker and those marked **(m)** by a male: those sections marked **(t)** should be read by the teacher.

(t) You are staying with your pen friend, Heike, in Germany.

Question number one.

What does Heike offer you for breakfast?

Tick **three** of the boxes.

(f)   **Was möchtest du zum Frühstück? Vati hat gerade frische Brötchen vom Bäcker geholt. Und vielleicht hast du Lust auf ein gekochtes Ei? Zu trinken haben wir nur Tee. Kaffee ist leider alle.**

(30 seconds)

(t) Question number two.

During breakfast Heike shows you a photo of her older brother, Ralf.

Which of the people in the photo is Ralf? Put a cross at the correct person.

(f)   **Das hier ist mein Bruder Ralf, als er beim Bäcker gearbeitet hat. Er ist der zweite von links, dahinten.**

(30 seconds)

(t) Question number three.

Today you are going to meet Heike's friend, Kirsten, and go to a country park. Heike makes two suggestions.

What does she suggest you do? Write **two** things.

(f)   **Wir kommen heute erst um 15 Uhr wieder nach Hause. Du solltest dir also etwas für das Mittagessen mitnehmen. Und es soll heute regnen—nimm lieber eine Jacke mit!**

(30 seconds)

(t) Question number four.

Heike says you will have to hurry.

Why will you have to hurry? Write **two** things.

(f) **Wir müssen uns beeilen. Ich habe mich für 10 Uhr mit meiner Freundin Kirsten am Busbahnhof verabredet. Der Bus fährt fünf Minuten später von dort ab.**

(30 seconds)

(t) Question number five.

You go with Heike and Kirsten to the country park. You go to buy the entrance tickets.

What will it cost for each of you?

What does the person who sells the tickets want to see?

(m) **Guten Tag! Erwachsene bezahlen fünf Mark, Schüler und Studenten drei Mark. Seid ihr Schüler? Ja? Kann ich bitte eure Schülerausweise sehen?**

(30 seconds)

(t) Question number six.

Heike tells you why she likes coming to the park.

What do Heike and Kirsten want to have as jobs later in life? Tick **one** box for Heike and **one** for Kirsten.

(f) **Ich komme oft zum Naturpark, weil ich mich sehr für Tiere interessiere. Ich möchte später als Tierärztin in so einem Park arbeiten. Und du möchtest den Leuten immer noch die Haare schneiden, Kirsten, nicht wahr?**

(30 seconds)

(t) Question number seven.

Kirsten has just been away on holiday with her family. She shows you a picture of where they stayed.

Put a tick in the correct box to show the hotel where they stayed.

(f) **Das Hotel, wo wir gewohnt haben, lag an einem kleinen See. Es gab sogar einen Sandstrand. Um das Hotel herum standen schöne große Bäume. Unser Zimmer war im dritten Stock.**

(30 seconds)

(t) Question number eight.

Kirsten tells you what she did on holiday.

Tick **two** of the boxes to show what **she** did while on holiday.

(f) **Uns war nie langweilig. Ich habe viel in der Sonne gelegen. Mein Vater hatte endlich Zeit zum Tennisspielen und ich konnte reiten gehen. Leider durfte ich nicht windsurfen.**

(30 seconds)

1997

(t) Question number nine.

Kirsten invites you and Heike to her house for a barbecue later that week.

When is the invitation for?

What is the reason for the barbecue? Write **two** things.

(f) **Wenn ihr beide Lust habt, könnt ihr am Donnerstagabend bei uns vorbeikommen. Es gibt eine Grillparty. Meine Schwester fährt für ein halbes Jahr als Au-pair nach Paris. Sie wird an ihrem Geburtstag nicht zu Hause sein.**

(30 seconds)

(t) Question number ten.

On the way home from the country park, Heike tells you about the classes she has at school the next day.

Why does she not like PE?

Why does she like Physics and Geography? Fill in the grid.

(f) **Morgen haben wir eine Doppelstunde Sport. Sport in der Schule finde ich recht langweilig. Physik haben wir morgen auch. Physik mache ich gerne. Mit Herrn Bauer, dem Physiklehrer, verstehe ich mich ganz gut. Und Erdkunde wird auch nicht schlecht sein. Das finde ich im Moment ganz interessant.**

(30 seconds)

(t) Question number eleven.

Heike tells you that she will have to stay in school the following afternoon.

Why does she have to stay in school?

(f) **Ich muß am Nachmittag in der Schule bleiben. Mein Englischlehrer hat eine Theatergruppe, und wir müssen von zwei Uhr bis halb vier üben.**

(30 seconds)

(t) Question number twelve.

Heike suggests what you could do the next afternoon while she is in school.

What could you do in the town? What can you do at the museum?

(f) **Du kannst natürlich mitkommen oder vielleicht würdest du lieber in die Stadt gehen. Wir haben ja schöne Geschäfte, wo du Geschenke für deine Familie kaufen kannst. Es gibt auch ein neues Heimatmuseum, wo man viel über die Geschichte der Stadt lernen kann.**

(30 seconds)

(t) Question number thirteen.

You agree that you will go into town the next day. Heike will meet you there later.

She wants to buy a new sleeping bag. What is wrong with her old sleeping bag? Write **two** things.

(f) **Ich muß mir in der Stadt einen neuen Schlafsack kaufen. Mein alter Schlafsack ist mir viel zu kurz—oder ich bin größer geworden! Außerdem ist er jetzt ein bißchen altmodisch. Die modernen Schlafsäcke sind viel besser.**

(30 seconds)

(t) End of test.

You now have 5 minutes to look over your answers.

[END OF TRANSCRIPT]

SCOTTISH
CERTIFICATE OF
EDUCATION
1997

WEDNESDAY, 28 MAY
1.00 PM – 1.25 PM
(APPROX)

GERMAN
STANDARD GRADE
General Level
Listening

When you are told to do so, open your paper.

You will hear a number of short items in German. You will hear each item twice, then you will have time to write your answer.

Write your answers, **in English**, in this book, in the appropriate spaces.

You may take notes as you are listening to the German, but only in this paper.

You may **not** use a German dictionary.

You are not allowed to leave the examination room until the end of the test.

Before leaving the examination room you must give this book to the invigilator. If you do not, you may lose all the marks for this paper.

You are staying with your pen friend, Heike, in Germany.

Marks

1. What does Heike offer you for breakfast? Tick (✓) **three** of the boxes.　　　**(3)**

	Tick (✓)
Bread	
Rolls	
Egg	
Cheese	
Tea	
Coffee	

*　　*　　*　　*　　*

2. During breakfast Heike shows you a photo of her older brother, Ralf.

   Which of the people in the photo is Ralf? Put a cross (✗) at the correct person.

(1)

Marks

3. Today you are going to meet Heike's friend, Kirsten, and go to a country park. Heike makes two suggestions.

What does she suggest you do? Write **two** things.   **(2)**

_____

_____

*   *   *   *   *

4. Heike says you will have to hurry.

Why will you have to hurry? Write **two** things.   **(2)**

_____

_____

*   *   *   *   *

5. You go with Heike and Kirsten to the country park. You go to buy the entrance tickets.

(*a*) What will it cost for each of you?   **(1)**

_____

(*b*) What does the person who sells the tickets want to see?   **(1)**

_____

*   *   *   *   *

6. Heike tells you why she likes coming to the park.

What do Heike and Kirsten want to have as jobs later in life? Tick (✓) **one** box for Heike and **one** for Kirsten.   **(2)**

	Heike	Kirsten
Doctor		
Vet		
Gardener		
Hairdresser		
Architect		

*   *   *   *   *

Marks

7. Kirsten has just been away on holiday with her family. She shows you a picture of where they stayed.

Put a tick (✓) in the correct box to show the hotel where they stayed. **(1)**

* * * * *

8. Kirsten tells you what she did on holiday.

Tick (✓) **two** of the boxes to show what **she** did while on holiday.   **(2)**

9. Kirsten invites you and Heike to her house for a barbecue later that week.

   (*a*) When is the invitation for? **(1)**

                               _____

   (*b*) What is the reason for the barbecue? Write **two** things. **(2)**

_____

_____

*   *   *   *   *

10. On the way home from the country park, Heike tells you about the classes she has at school the next day.

   (*a*) Why does she not like PE? **(1)**

   (*b*) Why does she like Physics and Geography?

       Fill in the grid. **(2)**

Physics	
Geography	

*   *   *   *   *

11. Heike tells you that she will have to stay in school the following afternoon.
Why does she have to stay in school? **(1)**

*   *   *   *   *

Marks

12. Heike suggests what you could do the next afternoon while she is in school.

(*a*) What could you do in the town? **(1)**

_____

(*b*) What can you do at the museum? **(1)**

_____

* * * * *

13. You agree that you will go into town the next day. Heike will meet you there later.

She wants to buy a new sleeping bag. What is wrong with her old sleeping bag? Write **two** things. **(2)**

_____

_____

* * * * *

Total (26)

[END OF QUESTION PAPER]

SCOTTISH
CERTIFICATE OF
EDUCATION
1997

FRIDAY, 30 MAY
9.30 AM – 10.15 AM

GERMAN
STANDARD GRADE
General Level
(Optional Paper)
Writing

When you are told to do so, open your paper and write your answers **in German** in the spaces provided.

You may use a German dictionary.

Before leaving the examination room you must give this book to the invigilator. If you do not, you may lose all the marks for this paper.

Your school is organising an exchange with a German school. Your teacher is gathering information to send to the German school.

Note: Examples are given to help you with ideas. These are only suggestions and you are free to use ideas of your own.

1. Your teacher asks you to write a few sentences about your family.

    You could mention, for example, where you live, how many there are in your family, how you get on with each other, etc. Write at least **three** sentences.

> Wir wohnen in Edinburg, in der Stadtmitte.
> Edinburg liegt im Sud-Ost an der Küste.
> Ich wohne mit meinen Eltern und meiner Schwester
> Mein Vater ist Zahnartzt
> Ich habe eine Gute Beziehung zu meiner Mutter.

2. You are asked to write about what you do in your spare time. (You could also mention something you don't like doing.) Write at least **three** sentences.

> Weil das Leben im Moment so stressig ist, mit Prüfungen und so weiter, daß in meiner Freizeit muß ich mich total entspannen.
>
> Am Wochenende gehe ich gern mit meinen Freundinnen aus, normalerweise gehe wir durch die Geschäfte, ich mache das gern, denn ich kann mir aussuchen, was ich mag.
>
> Auch spiele ich Klavier, darum muß ich dreißig Minuten pro Tag üben, daß finde ich ganz langweilig.
>
> Wenn ich Geld genug habe, gehe ich gern ins Theater.

3. Your teacher asks you to write down three questions you would like to ask your exchange partner about the place where they live.

You could ask, for example, how many people live there, what there is for young people to see and do, etc. Ask at least **three** questions.

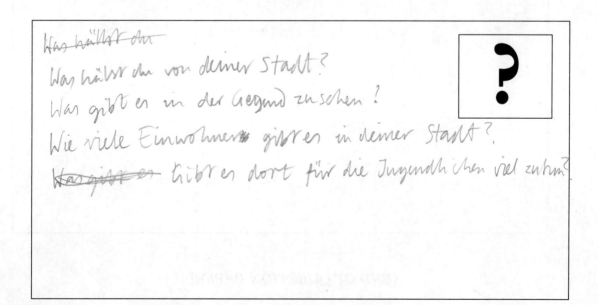

> ~~Was hältst du~~
>
> Was hälst du von deiner Stadt?
>
> Was gibt es in der Gegend zu sehen?
>
> Wie viele Einwohner gibt es in deiner Stadt?
>
> ~~Was gibt es~~ Gibt es dort für die Jugendlichen viel zu tun?

4. You are also asked to describe what you look like. You could mention height, colour and length of hair, colour of eyes, etc. Write at least **three** sentences.

Ich bin ziemlich klein.
Ich habe kurze, glatte, rote Haare.
Ich habe blaue Augen.

5. You are asked to write about a place you visited recently in your own area. (The German group might want to visit this place when they come to Scotland.)

You could mention, for example, where you went, how you got there, what you did there, etc. Write at least **three** sentences.

Vor einer Woche, bin ich mit meinen Freundinnen
nach Loch Leven gefahren.
~~Essen~~ Wir haben das Naturschutzgebiet besucht,
um interessante Vögel zu beobachten.
Am Nachmittag haben wir eine lange Wanderung
um dem See herum gemacht.
Zu Abend haben wir ein Picnick gegessen.
~~Wir haben~~ Es hat uns viel Spaß gemacht

[END OF QUESTION PAPER]

SCOTTISH
CERTIFICATE OF
EDUCATION
1998

TUESDAY, 26 MAY
G/C 9.15 AM –10.00 AM
F/G 10.00 AM –10.45 AM

**GERMAN
STANDARD GRADE**
General Level
Reading

When you are told to do so, open your paper and write your answers **in English** in the spaces provided. You may use a German dictionary.

Before leaving the examination room you must give this book to the invigilator. If you do not, you may lose all the marks for this paper.

You are staying with your German pen friend. One day you read a magazine.

1. In the magazine there is a competition. You have to guess the countries from the clues that are given. Here are the clues:

A

- Das Land grenzt an die Nordsee.

- Hier kann man am Markt bekannte Käsesorten kaufen.

B

- Das Land liegt auf einer Insel.

- Alle Autos, Lastwagen und Busse fahren auf der linken Straßenseite.

C

Marks

- Das ist das größte Land Europas.

- In der Hauptstadt sieht man diesen berühmten Turm.

D

- Aus diesem Land kommen die besten Uhren.

- Viele Urlauber kommen zum Wandern und Skilaufen hierher.

Choose **one** clue for each country and say what the clue is.

(4)

A Holland	
B Great Britain	
C France	
D Switzerland	

2. This article is about how much money different groups of people spend on holidays.

Singles reisen teurer

Was die Deutschen pro Person für eine
zweiwöchige Urlaubsreise ausgeben.

Jugendliche	1069DM
Junge Erwachsene	1311DM
Singles	2266DM
Paare	1792DM
Familie mit Kindern	1026DM
Familie mit Jugendlichen	1499DM
Rentner	1548DM

Put a tick (✓) in the correct box to show whether these statements are **True** or **False**.

(2)

	True	False
Families with young children spend more than families with teenagers.		
Pensioners spend least of all.		

3. This article is about open-air cinemas.

> # *Filme unter*
> # *freiem Himmel*
>
> Open-air Kinos sind in!
>
> Hier ein paar Tips, damit das open-air Kino noch mehr Spaß macht.
>
> ** Kissen mitbringen, aber bitte keine Stühle: Die sind nur im Weg.
>
> ** Picknickkorb nicht vergessen! Getränke und Würstchen gibt es fast überall, sie sind aber meist viel zu teuer.
>
> ** Einen Regenschirm braucht man auch. Ohne Regenschirm bei strömendem Regen macht keinen Spaß.

Tick (✓) **three** pieces of advice given in the article.

(3)

	Tick (✓)
Bring a chair to sit on.	
Wear warm clothes.	
Bring a cushion to sit on.	
Bring an umbrella.	
No umbrellas—they block the view for other people.	
Bring something to eat and drink.	

4. This article gives four tips for dealing with wasps.

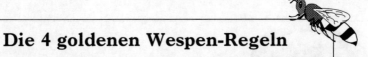

Die 4 goldenen Wespen-Regeln

1. Wespen lieben Cola-Dosen und dunkle Flaschen!
    Vorsicht beim Trinken!

2. Im Herbst nicht barfuß im Garten gehen. Zu dieser
    Zeit liegen die Wespen oft auf dem Erdboden!

3. Wespen hassen Zitronen! Legen Sie einfach eine
    Scheibe Zitrone auf das Fensterbrett, und die
    Wespen kommen nicht zu Besuch!

4. Versuchen Sie niemals, Wespennester selbst zu
    zerstören!

Choose any **three** of the tips and say what they are.

(3)

(a) _____

_____

(b) _____

_____

(c) _____

_____

5. Three young people write about a proposed ban on rollerblading in city centres.

Marks

Dieter

Ich finde Rollerblading sehr gefährlich in der Stadtmitte. Ich denke, zum Beispiel, an die Fußgängerzone. Man kann dort ältere Menschen sehr leicht überfahren.

Barbara

Inline-Skater bringen Leben in die toten Innenstädte und Fußgängerzonen. Mir macht es einfach Spaß, lautlos durch die Straßen zu gleiten.

Lisa

Ich fahre schon seit einem Jahr und bin noch nicht mit einem Fußgänger zusammengestoßen. Ich passe immer gut auf, wenn ich fahre. Ich finde es viel besser als mit dem Bus oder Auto zu fahren.

(*a*) Why is Dieter in favour of the ban? **(1)**

_____

_____

(*b*) Barbara and Lisa are against the ban. Why? Give **one** reason for each of them. **(2)**

Barbara: _____

_____

Lisa: _____

_____

Marks

6. In the magazine there are suggestions of games you could play on a long car journey. They are guessing games.

> ■ Welche Farbe hat das nächste Auto, das uns überholt?
>
> ■ Wie viele Leute sitzen im Auto hinter uns?
>
> ■ Mit welchem Buchstaben beginnt das Kennzeichen des nächsten Autos?
>
> ■ Ist der nächste Fußgänger auf der Straße Mann oder Frau, Junge oder Mädchen?

Choose any **three** of the games and explain clearly what they are.   **(3)**

(*a*) _____

_____

(*b*) _____

_____

(*c*) _____

_____

Marks

7. This article is about three young people and the sports they play.

CHRISTINE

Seit zwei Jahren schwimme ich in einem Verein. Mindestens zweimal die Woche trainiere ich, manchmal sogar viermal. Aber nur, wenn nicht zu viele Hausaufgaben zu machen sind. Hinterher bin ich immer sehr müde.

ANDREAS

Turnen mag ich am liebsten. Mit meiner Turngruppe nehme ich oft an Wettkämpfen teil. Dreimal habe ich schon den ersten Platz gemacht. Eine Medaille gab's auch! Wer turnen will, muß ein bißchen Mut haben.

MARIANNE

Ich spiele gern Fußball mit den Jungen. Wir spielen gegen andere Mannschaften. Manchmal verlieren wir, aber das macht uns nichts aus. Ich gehe jeden Samstag zu einem Fußballspiel. Dort schaue ich mir die Profis an, und probiere hinterher, was ich gesehen habe.

Write **one** name in each box to answer the questions.

(3)

	Name
Who tries to copy the experts?	
Who finds the training quite hard?	
Who has won competitions?	

8. In this article some young people say what they are worried about.

Marks

Was macht dir angst ?

Martina

Ich war eine Zeitlang im Ausland und jetzt verstehe ich mich mit meinen Freunden nicht mehr. Ich fühle mich jetzt ziemlich alleine.

Axel

Ich finde es schlimm, älter zu werden. Am liebsten würde ich nie älter als dreißig sein.

Hassan

Ich kann mir nichts Schlimmeres vorstellen, als den ganzen Tag im Büro zu sitzen und einen Job zu machen, der mir überhaupt keinen Spaß bringt.

Ilka

Manchmal habe ich Angst vor der Zukunft. Alles ist so ungewiß: Beruf, Wohnort, Geld und vieles andere.

What are these young people worried about? Write **one** thing for each person.

(4)

Martina	
Axel	
Hassan	
Ilka	

9. You read the headlines from four articles in the magazine.

1. # Traumjob
Ärztin
→ **Aber wie sieht das Studium aus?**

2. **MEDIZIN**
Kopfschmerzen hat jeder ab und zu—was hilft dagegen?

3. **Plötzlich bekommt das Leben eine neue Bedeutung**   **Karolina, 16, erbt ein Schloß** ↑

4. **„Danke schön, und bis zum nächsten Mal!"**
Jugendliche bringen Hilfsgüter nach Rußland

Choose any **three** of the headlines and explain clearly what the articles are about.

(3)

Headline Number	

10. One evening you go to a restaurant with your pen friend for a meal. After the meal you are asked to fill in this questionnaire.

> **Restaurant »Zum Spieß«**
>
> IHRE MEINUNG ist uns WICHTIG!
>
> **1. Wie oft kommen Sie zu diesem Restaurant?**
>
> ☐ erstmalig   ☐ mindestens einmal pro Woche
>
> ☐ mehrmals im Jahr   ☐ mehrmals im Monat
>
> ___
>
> **2. Wie ist Ihre Meinung nach dem heutigen Besuch?**
>
> | | zufrieden | unzufrieden |
> |---|---|---|
> | über das Essen | ☐ | ☐ |
> | über die Bedienung | ☐ | ☐ |
> | über den Preis | ☐ | ☐ |

This is the first time you have been to this restaurant. You find the food is good, but the service is slow and the meal is too expensive.

(a) Give your answer to the first question by putting a cross in the correct box. **(1)**

(b) Give your answers to the second question by putting a cross in **one** box in each row. **(3)**

Total (32)

[*END OF QUESTION PAPER*]

SCOTTISH
CERTIFICATE OF
EDUCATION
1998

TUESDAY, 26 MAY
11.45 AM – 12.10 PM
(APPROX)

GERMAN
STANDARD GRADE
General Level
Listening Transcript

Transcript—General Level

> **Instructions to reader(s):**
>
> For each item, read the English **once,** then read the German **twice,** with an interval of 7 seconds between the two readings. On completion of the second reading, pause for the length of time indicated in brackets after each item, to allow the candidates to write their answers.
>
> Where special arrangements have been agreed in advance to allow the reading of the material, those sections marked **(f)** should be read by a female speaker and those marked **(m)** by a male: those sections marked **(t)** should be read by the teacher.

(t) You are going with your pen friend, Thomas, to visit his cousin, Gisela, in Hameln.

(f) or (m)   **Du fährst mit deinem Brieffreund Thomas nach Hameln. Dort besucht ihr seine Kusine Gisela.**

(t) Question number one.

Thomas tells you how you are going to get there. Part of your journey will be by train.

Tick **two** of the boxes to show which other forms of transport you will use.

(m)   **Wir müssen mit der U-Bahn Linie 10 zum Hauptbahnhof fahren. Dann geht's mit der Bahn weiter nach Hameln. Dort holt uns meine Kusine Gisela mit ihrem Auto ab. Sie fährt uns dann zu ihrer Familie.**

(30 seconds)

(t) Question number two.

Thomas wants to buy a present for his aunt.

What **two** suggestions does he make? Tick **two** of the boxes.

(m)   **Wir müssen meiner Tante etwas mitbringen. Sie liest gerne. Ich glaube, ich kaufe ihr etwas zu lesen. Oder wir können ihr etwas Süßes zu essen kaufen, eine Schachtel Pralinen vielleicht?**

(30 seconds)

(t) Question number three.

You arrive at the station. Thomas asks about the train times to Hameln.

Tick the correct departure time and platform.

(m)   **Der nächste Zug nach Hameln fährt gleich um 10.45 Uhr von Gleis 7 ab. Sie müssen sich aber beeilen.**

(30 seconds)

(t) Question number four.

As you head for the train you hear the following announcement.

Why does someone have to go to the information desk?

(f) **Achtung! Achtung! Ein schwarzer Koffer ist auf Bahnsteig vier gefunden worden.**
or **Wer diesen Koffer verloren hat, soll sich bitte an der Information am Eingang des**
(m) **Bahnhofs melden. Danke!**

(30 seconds)

(t) Question number five.

You arrive in Hameln. Thomas's cousin, Gisela, meets you.

Put a tick at the **two** places Gisela must go to on the way home.

(f) **Hallo, ihr beide. Also, auf geht's nach Hause! Zuerst muß ich noch an der**
Tankstelle vorbei. Mein Benzin ist fast alle. Ich muß aber auch zur Apotheke.
Für Vati soll ich Medikamente abholen.

(30 seconds)

(t) Question number six.

Gisela tells you about where she lives.

Write **three** things she says.

(f) **Wir wohnen auf dem Land. Es dauert ungefähr zwanzig Minuten, bis wir da sind.**
Das Haus liegt direkt an einem schönen, kleinen See. Dort kann man prima
angeln gehen.

(30 seconds)

(t) Question number seven.

You arrive at Gisela's house and meet her mother. She welcomes you.

Gisela's father is a doctor.

Where is he? What has happened?

(f) **Herzlich willkommen hier bei uns! Ich hoffe, ihr hattet eine gute Reise. Mein**
Mann kommt erst später nach Hause. Er ist Arzt und mußte schnell in die Stadt
zu einem alten Patienten, der im Haus gefallen ist.

(30 seconds)

(t) Question number eight.

Gisela's mother takes you to meet her other daughter, Ingrid.

What is Ingrid doing?

(f) **Komm mit! Ingrid ist im Garten. Sie deckt den Tisch für das Abendessen. Wir**
wollen heute abend draußen essen.

(30 seconds)

中文

(t) Question number nine.

Gisela discusses her plans for the evening.

What are her plans? Write **two** things.

(f) Ich gehe heute Abend ins Kino. Es läuft zur Zeit ein toller Abenteuerfilm. Habt ihr Lust mitzukommen? Danach treffe ich mich mit meinen Freunden in der Stadtmitte.

(30 seconds)

(t) Question number ten.

That evening you meet Dieter, one of Gisela's friends.

He tells you about his plans for after the summer holidays.

What is Dieter planning to do? What **two** things does he ask you?

(m) Hallo, ich habe gerade gehört, du kommst aus Schottland. Nach den Sommerferien werde ich für drei Monate eine Schule in Edinburg besuchen. Wohnst du weit von dort? Können wir uns vielleicht an einem Wochenende treffen?

(30 seconds)

(t) Question number eleven.

Later that evening you talk about what you are going to do the next day. Gisela has some ideas.

What does she suggest doing if the weather is good? Write **two** things.

(f) Ich weiß nicht, wie das Wetter morgen wird. Wenn es schön ist, können wir eine Radtour machen. Wir haben Fahrräder. Wir können auf dem Land ein Picknick machen.

(30 seconds)

(t) Question number twelve.

What does she suggest doing if it is wet? Write **two** things.

(f) Falls es regnet, können wir immer noch ins Einkaufszentrum gehen. Ich brauche ein paar Hefte für die Schule. Dann könnten wir ins Heimatmuseum gehen. Das ist ganz interessant.

(30 seconds)

(t) Question number thirteen.

Gisela tells you what her friend Dieter has arranged for Saturday evening.

What has been planned? Write **two** things.

(f) Samstagabend sind wir um 6.00 Uhr bei meinem Freund Dieter zum Abendessen eingeladen. Er hat außerdem noch Karten für das Theater. Wir werden das Theaterstück „Der Rattenfänger von Hameln" sehen. Das wird bestimmt Spaß machen!

(30 seconds)

(t) End of test.

You now have 5 minutes to look over your answers.

[END OF TRANSCRIPT]

SCOTTISH
CERTIFICATE OF
EDUCATION
1998

TUESDAY, 26 MAY
11.45 AM – 12.10 PM
(APPROX)

GERMAN
STANDARD GRADE
General Level
Listening

When you are told to do so, open your paper.

You will hear a number of short items in German. You will hear each item twice, then you will have time to write your answer.

Write your answers, **in English**, in this book, in the appropriate spaces.

You may take notes as you are listening to the German, but only in this paper.

You may **not** use a German dictionary.

You are not allowed to leave the examination room until the end of the test.

Before leaving the examination room you must give this book to the invigilator. If you do not, you may lose all the marks for this paper.

You are going with your pen friend, Thomas, to visit his cousin, Gisela, in Hameln.

Du fährst mit deinem Brieffreund Thomas nach Hameln. Dort besucht ihr seine Kusine Gisela.

1. Thomas tells you how you are going to get there. Part of your journey will be by train.

   Tick (✓) **two** of the boxes to show which other forms of transport you will use.   **(2)**

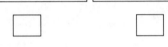

   ☐   ☐   ☐   ☐

   *   *   *   *   *

2. Thomas wants to buy a present for his aunt.

   What **two** suggestions does he make? Tick (✓) **two** of the boxes.   **(2)**

	Tick (✓)
Flowers	
A bottle of wine	
A book or magazine	
Biscuits	
Chocolates	

   *   *   *   *   *

3. You arrive at the station. Thomas asks about the train times to Hameln.

   Tick (✓) the correct departure time and platform.

   (*a*) Departure time: 10.45 ☐   11.15 ☐   11.45 ☐   **(1)**

   (*b*) Platform: 5 ☐   7 ☐   9 ☐   **(1)**

   *   *   *   *   *

4. As you head for the train you hear the following announcement.

Why does someone have to go to the information desk? **(1)**

_____

* * * * *

5. You arrive in Hameln. Thomas's cousin, Gisela, meets you.

Put a tick (✓) at the **two** places Gisela must go to on the way home. **(2)**

	Tick (✓)
Library	
Petrol Station	
Supermarket	
Chemist	
Baker	

* * * * *

6. Gisela tells you about where she lives.

Write **three** things she says. **(3)**

_____

_____

_____

* * * * *

7. You arrive at Gisela's house and meet her mother. She welcomes you.

Gisela's father is a doctor.

(*a*) Where is he? **(1)**

_____

(*b*) What has happened? **(1)**

_____

* * * * *

8. Gisela's mother takes you to meet her other daughter, Ingrid.

What is Ingrid doing? **(1)**

_____

* * * * *

9. Gisela discusses her plans for the evening.

What are her plans? Write **two** things. **(2)**

_____

_____

* * * * *

10. That evening you meet Dieter, one of Gisela's friends.

He tells you about his plans for after the summer holidays.

(*a*) What is Dieter planning to do? **(1)**

_____

(*b*) What **two** things does he ask you? **(2)**

_____

_____

* * * * *

11. Later that evening you talk about what you are going to do the next day. Gisela has some ideas.

What does she suggest doing if the weather is good? Write **two** things. **(2)**

_____

_____

* * * * *

12. What does she suggest doing if it is wet? Write **two** things. **(2)**

_____

_____

*   *   *   *   *

13. Gisela tells you what her friend Dieter has arranged for Saturday evening.
What has been planned? Write **two** things. **(2)**

_____

_____

*   *   *   *   *

Total (26)

[END OF QUESTION PAPER]

SCOTTISH
CERTIFICATE OF
EDUCATION
1998

TUESDAY, 26 MAY
1.50 PM – 2.35 PM

GERMAN
STANDARD GRADE
General Level
(Optional Paper)
Writing

When you are told to do so, open your paper and write your answers **in German** in the spaces provided.

You may use a German dictionary.

Before leaving the examination room you must give this book to the invigilator. If you do not, you may lose all the marks for this paper.

As part of a school project, your class is exchanging information with a school in Germany. Each pupil in your class has a German partner.

Note: Examples are given to help you with ideas. These are only suggestions and you are free to use ideas of your own.

1. You have to write about a typical school day. You could say when school starts and finishes, where you have your lunch, when you do your homework, how much homework you have, etc. Write at least **three** sentences.

2. In this section you ask your partner about school subjects. You could ask what subjects they take, what their favourite subject is, what they don't like studying, what the teachers are like, etc. Ask at least **three** questions.

?

3. Write about the things you do after school and at weekends. You could mention any hobbies or interests you have, what you do with your friends, where you go, etc. Write at least **three** sentences.

4. The German school is planning a visit to Scotland in three months' time. Write about what there is to see and do in your area. Write at least **three** sentences.

5. The German school has sent information on how German teenagers celebrate their birthday. Explain how you usually celebrate **your** birthday. You could say when your birthday is and write about the kind of presents you get, what you do on your birthday, etc. Write at least **three** sentences.

[END OF QUESTION PAPER]

SCOTTISH
CERTIFICATE OF
EDUCATION
1995

TUESDAY, 23 MAY
11.20 AM – 12.20 PM

GERMAN
STANDARD GRADE
Credit Level
Reading

Instructions to the Candidate

When you are told to do so, open your paper and write your answers **in English** in the **separate** answer book provided.

You may use a German dictionary.

Your German pen friend has sent you a magazine.

1. This is an article about one of Germany's young swimming stars.

Franziska von Almsick

„Ich bleibe, wie ich bin!"

Vor den Olympischen Spielen 1992 war Franziska von Almsick noch ein Mädchen wie alle andere. Nur schwimmen konnte sie um einiges besser. Davon nahmen aber nur wenige Notiz. Doch dann gewann die Vierzehnjährige eine Medaille nach der anderen, insgesamt vier.

Franziska war über Nacht berühmt. Nach ihrem Erfolg wollte jede Zeitschrift von ihr ein Interview. Wenn sie nicht gerade im Wasser war, wurde sie von Reportern bedrängt.

Franziska ist nicht nur berühmt geworden, sondern auch reich. Mit der Werbung für Schokolade oder Badeanzüge hat sie bereits über eine Million verdient. Da ist es gar nicht so leicht, normal zu bleiben. Auch auf der Straße gibt es für sie Probleme. Sie wird dauernd erkannt und angesprochen. Franziska meint: „Ich stehe jetzt im Vordergrund und ich fühle mich dauernd beobachtet."

Marks

(a) How successful was Franziska at the last Olympics? **(1)**

(b) What problems has Franziska had since her success at the last Olympics? (Write **three** things.) **(3)**

The article goes on to describe Franziska's training schedule.

Im Wasser fühlt sich Franziska immer noch am wohlsten. Ihr Ziel ist, noch schneller zu schwimmen, alles andere ist ihr nicht so wichtig. Und dafür arbeitet sie schon seit zehn Jahren jeden Tag hart. Morgens um sieben ist Trainingsbeginn in der Schwimmhalle der Sportschule. Franziska pflügt durch das Wasser, Bahn um Bahn, Kilometer um Kilometer. Nach dem Training hat Franziska Unterricht, am Nachmittag ist zum zweiten Mal Training angesagt. Schwimmen, schwimmen, schwimmen . . . Viel Zeit für anderes bleibt da kaum.

Marks

(c)   What is Franziska's schedule each day? (Write **three** things.)   **(3)**

2. A young Syrian girl, Rania, talks about her life in Germany. She and her family are refugees hoping to settle in Germany.

Meine Zukunft ist sehr ungewiß!

„Vor vier Jahren mußten wir plötzlich aus Syrien weg. Mein Vater hat bei einer Zeitung gearbeitet. Er hat eine andere Meinung vertreten als die der Regierung. Er und sein Freund wurden politisch verfolgt. Wir sind dann nach Deutschland geflüchtet. Zuerst waren wir in einem Flüchtlingslager. Später sind wir in unsere Wohnung gekommen. Meine Eltern hoffen, daß die deutschen Behörden uns bald Asyl geben. Solange wir kein Asyl kriegen, dürfen meine Eltern hier nicht arbeiten.

Das macht meiner Mama nichts aus, sie versorgt ja mich und meine Schwester Ninawe. Ninawe ist jetzt sechs. Aber mein Vater sagt: „Ich bin zu jung zum Spazierengehen wie ein Rentner." Er sagt: „Lange halte ich das nicht mehr aus."

Meine Eltern sind trotzdem gerne in Deutschland. Sie haben hier nette Leute kennengelernt. Aber wenn wir nicht bald Asyl bekommen, wollen meine Eltern nach Australien. Dort leben viele Verwandte von uns. Meine Schwester und ich wollen aber lieber in Deutschland bleiben. Deutsch können wir inzwischen sehr gut. Ich möchte hier gerne weiter zur Schule gehen. Später einmal will ich Ärztin werden. Hier in Deutschland gibt es für Ärzte bessere Berufschancen. Aber meine Zukunft ist sehr ungewiß. Eigentlich mag ich gar nicht daran denken."

Marks

(a) Why did Rania's family have to leave Syria? Write **two** things. **(2)**

(b) Where have they lived since they came to Germany? Write **two** things. **(2)**

(c) Her parents are not allowed to work until they have been granted asylum.
How does the mother react to this? Write **two** things.
How does the father react to this? Write **two** things. **(4)**

(d) Why do Rania and her sister want to stay in Germany? Write **three** things. **(3)**

3. A girl called Marita feels her parents do not understand her. She expresses her feelings
    in this poem.

Eltern

Ihr wollt gute Eltern sein,
aber Ihr tut das Falsche.
Warum seht Ihr
meine Tränen nicht,
die ich in der Hoffnung weine,
daß Ihr mich tröstet?
Oder wollt Ihr sie nicht sehen?
Ihr wart auch einmal so jung wie ich.
Könnt Ihr Euch nicht erinnern,
daß Ihr auch solche Probleme hattet?
Oder wollt Ihr es nur nicht?
Bitte, helft mir,
sonst werden diese Gefühle
mich zersprengen.
Bitte, lacht mich nicht aus,
nehmt mich ernst!
Nehmt Euch Zeit
mit mir zu sprechen!
Sonst wird meine Verzweiflung
umso tiefer
wegen dieser Gefühle.

Marita (17 Jahre)

Marks

(*a*)   What does Marita criticise her parents for? Write **three** things.   (3)

(*b*)   She asks them for help.
        What **three** things could they do to help?   (3)

4. Some young people talk about their friends. They say what is important in their friendships and what problems they have had with friends.

Mit meinen Freunden Nils und Lars kann ich über alles reden. Auch, wenn ich Probleme mit meiner Freundin Michaela habe. So ein Gespräch kommt meistens ganz spontan. Einer fängt an, dann erzählen die anderen von ihren Erfahrungen, und so geht das weiter. Wir haben uns auch schon gestritten. Da war ein halbes Jahr, wo wir uns gar nicht getroffen haben. Jeder war zu stolz, um sich zu entschuldigen. Ich glaube, die besten Freunde findet man in der Schulzeit. Danach habe ich kaum noch jemanden kennengelernt. Wir sind immer in der alten Clique zusammen. Ein oder zwei Neue sind dazugekommen, aber mit denen entwickelt sich nie so eine dicke Freundschaft.

Dirk, 18 Jahre

Michaela, 19 Jahre

Für mich ist mein Freund wichtiger, als meine beste Freundin. Ich habe Vertrauen zu ihm. Man kann immer zu ihm kommen. Dirk habe ich in der Disko kennengelernt. Er hat mich angesprochen. Wir kennen uns seit drei Jahren. Seit eineinhalb Jahren sind wir verlobt. Als ich Dirk kennengelernt habe, bekam ich Probleme mit meiner besten Freundin. Sie war enttäuscht, daß ich keine Zeit mehr für sie hatte. Sie hat hinter meinem Rücken über mich geredet. Dirk und ich haben gleiche Interessen, machen alles zusammen. Auch die Clique ist sehr wichtig. Man braucht Freunde. Wir sind fast jeden Abend zusammen.

Wir Mädchen in der Clique sind ziemlich gute Freundinnen. Mit Alexandra kann ich auch über Probleme reden, die nicht die Clique betreffen. Solche Themen muß nicht jeder hören. Eine andere Freundin hat mich einmal sehr enttäuscht. Ich hab' ihr mal etwas privat erzählt, und das hat sie dann in der Clique weitererzählt. Ich hatte dann nachher große Schwierigkeiten, mit der Clique über andere Probleme zu reden.

Heike, 17 Jahre

Marks

(a) What is important in their friendships? Write **one** thing for each person. **(3)**

(b) What problems have they had in their friendships? Choose **two** of the young people and write **two** things for each. **(4)**

Total **(31)**

[END OF QUESTION PAPER]

SCOTTISH
CERTIFICATE OF
EDUCATION
1995

TUESDAY, 23 MAY
3.10 PM – 3.40 PM
(APPROX)

GERMAN
STANDARD GRADE
Credit Level
Listening Transcript

Instructions to reader(s):

For each item, read the English **once,** then read the German **twice**, with an interval of 7 seconds between the two readings. On completion of the second reading, pause for the length of time indicated in brackets after each item, to allow the candidates to write their answers.

Where special arrangements have been agreed in advance by the Board to allow the reading of the material, those sections marked **(f)** should be read by a female speaker and those sections marked **(m)** by a male: those sections marked **(t)** should be read by the teacher.

(t) You are staying with your friend Friedrich at his home on the North German island of Nordstrand. Friedrich used to live in Hamburg and moved to Nordstrand only three years ago. One evening you get together with some of his friends.

Question number one.

One of Friedrich's friends asks him how he likes living on Nordstrand.

Why does Friedrich prefer Nordstrand to Hamburg? Give **three** reasons.

(m)   **Ja, mir gefällt es hier auf Nordstrand sehr gut. Ich lebe gern hier direkt am Meer. In Hamburg waren die Autos immer so laut und haben die Luft ziemlich stark verschmutzt. Hier ist es viel ruhiger und die Luft ist frisch und sauber. Am besten ist es aber, daß ich auf Nordstrand mehr Freunde habe als in Hamburg.**

(40 seconds)

(t) Question number two.

His friend asks him if he misses anything about Hamburg.

What does Friedrich miss about Hamburg? Write **two** things.

(m)   **Ja, ein bißchen schon. Zum Beispiel hier auf Nordstrand fehlt es an guten Geschäften. Die gibt es in Husum aber das ist zwanzig Minuten von hier entfernt. Da kann man gut einkaufen gehen. Außerdem haben wir auch nicht die Möglichkeit, so leicht und schnell in andere deutsche Großstädte zu kommen. Vom Hamburger Hauptbahnhof aus konnte ich in vier Stunden Städte wie Köln oder Leipzig erreichen.**

(40 seconds)

(t) Question number three.

Another friend asks him if he wants to stay on Nordstrand when he leaves school.

What do the young people of Nordstrand do when they leave school? Write **three** things.

(m) Ja, ich möchte auch später auf Nordstrand bleiben. Aber es ist sehr schwer, hier eine Stelle zu finden. Hier in der Gegend arbeiten die meisten jungen Leute auf einem Bauernhof oder sie arbeiten in den vielen Gasthöfen und Hotels. Sonst steht es schlecht mit Arbeitsstellen. Wie du weißt, finden viele keine Stelle und müssen nach Süddeutschland. Wenn ich eine gute Stelle finde, kann ich vielleicht hier bleiben. Auf keinen Fall möchte ich im Tourismusbereich arbeiten.

(40 seconds)

(t) Question number four.

Friedrich's parents work in the tourist industry.

How does this affect Friedrich? Write **two** things.

(m) Meine Eltern vermieten seit zwei Jahren Zimmer an Feriengäste. Von März bis Oktober hat meine Mutter nur mit Gästen zu tun. Oft muß ich meiner Mutter helfen, wenn ich lieber ausgehen möchte. Meine Eltern haben auch nie Zeit, sich mit mir zu unterhalten. Wenn ich einmal Kinder habe, möchte ich mehr Zeit für sie haben, als meine Eltern für mich hatten.

(40 seconds)

(t) Question number five.

His parents' guest house has been very successful.

How do his parents plan to spend the money they earn from the guest house? Write **three** things.

(m) Meine Eltern vermieten dieses Jahr noch mehr Zimmer als letztes Jahr. Das machen sie, weil die Touristen soviel Geld mitbringen. Mein Vater will sich bald ein neues Auto kaufen. Außerdem fliegen sie jedes Jahr im November nach Tunesien in den Urlaub, und sie haben mir versprochen, die Kosten meines Studiums an der Universität zu bezahlen.

(40 seconds)

(t) Question number six.

The German you have heard spoken by some of the local people sounds unusual. Sabine, one of Friedrich's friends, explains why.

Why is the dialect of this area used less nowadays? Give **three** reasons.

(f) Ja, wir sprechen hier einen Dialekt. Man nennt das Plattdeutsch. Früher haben die Leute hier nur Plattdeutsch gesprochen, aber in letzter Zeit sprechen die Kinder viel weniger unseren Dialekt. Ein Grund dafür ist der Kontakt mit den vielen Touristen. In der Schule wird der Dialekt selten gebraucht, und im Fernsehen kommen auch nur wenige Sendungen im Dialekt.

(40 seconds)

(t) Question number seven.

The young people talk about the number of foreign people who have moved into the area and the problems there have been. Sabine gives her opinion.

What difficulty do foreign people have when they move to an area like Nordstrand? Write **one** thing.

What ideas does she have to help them? Write **two** things.

(f)   Für Ausländer ist es gar nicht einfach, sich hier einzuleben. Ich finde, wir müssen ihnen helfen. Nur wenn sie unsere Freunde werden, können sie sich hier wohl fühlen. Auf Nordstrand ist es schwer für diese Menschen, Freunde zu finden. Vielleicht sollten wir die jungen Leute in den Jugendklub einladen. Wir könnten auch eine Party für die Familien veranstalten.

(40 seconds)

(t) Question number eight.

Jan, another of Friedrich's friends, agrees with Sabine.

Who has Jan met recently? Why has this person not yet made any friends?

(m)   Ja klar, wir müssen den ersten Schritt machen. Ich kenne einen Jungen aus Rußland. Er ist mit seiner Familie vor drei Wochen nach Nordstrand gekommen. Sein Deutsch ist nicht sehr gut. Kein Wunder also, wenn er im Moment keine deutschen Freunde hat.

(40 seconds)

(t) Question number nine.

Jan and Sabine plan to help this person make friends.

What does Jan say he is going to do? Write **two** things.

What does Sabine offer to do? Write **two** things.

(m)   Jan: Also, gut, ich werde ihn morgen ansprechen. Vielleicht möchte er am Donnerstag abend zum Handballtraining kommen.

(f)   Sabine: Ja, und nachher könnt ihr alle zu mir kommen. Ich werde die beiden ausländischen Mädchen aus dem Dorf einladen. Wir können uns bei einer guten Tasse Kaffee kennenlernen.

(40 seconds)

(t) End of test.

You now have 5 minutes to look over your answers.

[END OF TRANSCRIPT]

SCOTTISH
CERTIFICATE OF
EDUCATION
1995

TUESDAY, 23 MAY
3.10 PM – 3.40 PM
(APPROX)

GERMAN
STANDARD GRADE
Credit Level
Listening

Instructions to the Candidate

When you are told to do so, open your paper.

You will hear a number of short items in German. You will hear each item twice, then you will have time to write your answer.

Write your answers, **in English**, in the **separate** answer book provided.

You may take notes as you are listening to the German, but only in your answer book.

You may **not** use a German dictionary.

You are not allowed to leave the examination room until the end of the test.

Marks

You are staying with your friend Friedrich at his home on the North German island of Nordstrand. Friedrich used to live in Hamburg and moved to Nordstrand only three years ago. One evening you get together with some of his friends.

1. One of Friedrich's friends asks him how he likes living on Nordstrand.
    Why does Friedrich prefer Nordstrand to Hamburg? Give **three** reasons. **(3)**

    *   *   *   *   *

2. His friend asks him if he misses anything about Hamburg.
    What does Friedrich miss about Hamburg? Write **two** things. **(2)**

    *   *   *   *   *

3. Another friend asks him if he wants to stay on Nordstrand when he leaves school.
    What do the young people of Nordstrand do when they leave school? Write **three** things. **(3)**

    *   *   *   *   *

4. Friedrich's parents work in the tourist industry.
    How does this affect Friedrich? Write **two** things. **(2)**

    *   *   *   *   *

5. His parents' guest house has been very successful.

How do his parents plan to spend the money they earn from the guest house? Write **three** things. **(3)**

*   *   *   *   *

6. The German you have heard spoken by some of the local people sounds unusual. Sabine, one of Friedrich's friends, explains why.

Why is the dialect of this area used less nowadays? Give **three** reasons. **(3)**

*   *   *   *   *

7. The young people talk about the number of foreign people who have moved into the area and the problems there have been.

Sabine gives her opinion.

(*a*) What difficulty do foreign people have when they move to an area like Nordstrand? Write **one** thing. **(1)**

(*b*) What ideas does she have to help them? Write **two** things. **(2)**

*   *   *   *   *

8. Jan, another of Friedrich's friends, agrees with Sabine.

(*a*) Who has Jan met recently? **(1)**

(*b*) Why has this person not yet made any friends? **(1)**

*   *   *   *   *

9. Jan and Sabine plan to help this person make friends.

(*a*) What does Jan say he is going to do? Write **two** things. **(2)**

(*b*) What does Sabine offer to do? Write **two** things. **(2)**

*   *   *   *   *

Total (25)

[END OF QUESTION PAPER]

GERMAN STANDARD GRADE
Credit Level
(Optional Paper)
Writing

Blauer Himmel! Sonnenschein! Ferien!

The following young German people were asked how they spend their summer holidays.

Im letzten Herbst habe ich meine Brieffreundin Hanna in Prag besucht. Das war ein sehr billiger Urlaub, weil ich bei ihrer Familie kostenlos gewohnt habe. Nur die Reise mit dem Zug mußte ich bezahlen. Hanna hat mir viel von Land und Leuten gezeigt. Ich habe viel Neues durch meine Reise gelernt.

Heike, 15 Jahre

Ich fahre am liebsten dorthin, wo Sonne ist. Mit meinen Eltern bin ich im letzten Sommer nach Teneriffa geflogen. Dort haben wir zwei Wochen lang in einem Hotel gewohnt. Jeden Tag war ich am Strand und habe gebadet oder mich gesonnt. Abends bin ich in verschiedenen Diskos gewesen. Es war niemals langweilig.

Max, 15 Jahre

Mein letzter Urlaub war super! Endlich konnte ich mit meiner Freundin allein verreisen. Wir wollten eine Tour mit Zelten und Rädern machen, weil wir nicht viel Geld hatten. Zuerst mußten wir eine Reiseroute planen. Zum Glück gab es wenig Probleme mit dem Wetter und den Fahrrädern. Wir hatten viel Spaß und endlich einmal Ruhe von den Eltern!

Detler, 17 Jahre

Im letzten Jahr bin ich gar nicht in Urlaub gefahren, sondern bin die ganze Zeit zu Hause geblieben. Dort kann ich solange ausschlafen, wie ich will. In den Ferien hatte ich viel Zeit für Star, mein eigenes Pferd. Ich bin oft mit meiner besten Freundin ausgeritten. Manchmal habe ich bei meiner Freundin übernachtet.

Hannah, 16 Jahre

Now it's your turn!

Here are some questions you may wish to consider. You do not have to use all of them, and you are free to include other relevant ideas.

*   How do you spend your summer holidays?

*   When you are at home, what do you do in your holidays?

*   Where did you go the last time you went away?

*   If you had the choice, where would you like to spend a holiday?

Write about 200 words **in German**. You may use a German dictionary.

[END OF QUESTION PAPER]

SCOTTISH
CERTIFICATE OF
EDUCATION
1996

TUESDAY, 28 MAY
11.20 AM – 12.20 PM

GERMAN
STANDARD GRADE
Credit Level
Reading

Instructions to the Candidate

When you are told to do so, open your paper and write your answers **in English** in the **separate** answer book provided.

You may use a German dictionary.

Your German pen friend has sent you a magazine.

1. This article gives advice on taking your pets with you on holiday.

Mit Hund und Katze im Urlaub?

Immer mehr Familien nehmen ihr Tier mit in die Ferien. Man kann endlich einmal mit ihm zusammen wandern, schwimmen und herumtollen.

Am einfachsten ist das Verreisen mit dem Hund im eigenen Auto. Hunde lassen sich gerne durch die Gegend fahren. Auf langen Fahrten sollte man dem Hund die Möglichkeit geben, zwischendurch die Beine strecken zu können—am Rande großer Straßen selbstverständlich nur an der Leine. Und sollte Ihr Hund zu den wenigen gehören, die das Autofahren nicht vertragen, so wird der Tierarzt gerne Tabletten gegen Reisekrankheit verschreiben.

Wenn Katzenbesitzer Urlaubspläne machen, sollen sie bedenken, daß die meisten Katzen nicht gerne verreisen. Ungewohnte Umgebungen sind für Katzen kein Vergnügen. Die beste Lösung heißt daher: Die Katze bleibt zu Hause.

Marks

(a) Why do more and more families take their pet on holiday? **(1)**

(b) What **two** pieces of advice are given to people who decide to take their dog with them in the car? **(2)**

(c) You are advised to leave your cat at home. Why? **(1)**

Marks

More and more hotels are happy to welcome dogs as guests.

Hotels, in denen Hunde willkommen sind, gibt es übrigens immer häufiger. Wie ein Hoteldirektor einmal bemerkte, „Hunde putzen sich nicht mit den Vorhängen die Schuhe, brennen keine Löcher in den Teppich und nehmen auch nicht den Aschenbecher als Souvenir mit."

(*d*)   Why are hotel managers happy to have dogs as guests? Write **three** things.   **(3)**

Marks

2. Three young people write about growing up.

Suzanne, who is 17, has very positive feelings about growing up.

> Ich habe gute Erfahrungen mit dem Erwachsenwerden gemacht. Das liegt wahrscheinlich daran, daß ich mit meinen Eltern über alle Probleme sprechen kann. Man bekommt immer mehr Rechte. Mit achtzehn kann man den Führerschein machen und wählen gehen.

Suzanne

(*a*) Why does Susanne feel positive about growing up? Write **three** things. **(3)**

Marco, who is 16, is more negative about growing up.

> Angst habe ich davor, daß später nichts aus mir wird, daß ich keinen Beruf finde und daß ich die Verantwortung für eine eigene Familie nicht tragen kann. Manchmal habe ich auch Angst, daß die Partnerschaft und das Leben langweilig werden.

Marco

(*b*) What are his fears for the future? Write **three** things. **(3)**

Nicole (also 16) has mixed feelings about growing up.

Erwachsenwerden ist für mich die Chance, sich von Freunden und Eltern zu lösen und einen eigenen Weg zu finden, nicht mehr abhängig zu sein. Manchmal behandeln meine Eltern mich wie ein Kind, wenn ich am Wochenende ausgehen möchte. Sie geben mir keinen Freiraum.

Nicole

(c) Write **one** positive thing she says about growing up and **one** negative thing.

(2)

Marks

3. You read an article about careers for young people.

> **Es gibt heute viele Berufe, die den Jugendlichen offen stehen. Da ist es oft schwierig, die richtige Wahl zu treffen. Diese Fragen muß jeder Jugendliche sich selbst beantworten: Kann ich meine Interessen einbringen? Welche Zukunfts- und Aufstiegschancen habe ich?**
>
> **In Deutschland entscheiden sich 85 Prozent der Mädchen für nur 15 Berufe. Entscheidend sind hier sicher das Elternhaus und die Schule—in der Regel wird einfach noch sehr traditionell gedacht. Mädchen brauchen mehr Ermutigung durch Eltern und Lehrer.**

(*a*) What two questions should young people ask themselves when choosing a career? Write **two** things.   **(2)**

(*b*) Girls in Germany tend to choose a limited number of jobs. What reason is given for this?   **(1)**

(*c*) What can be done to change this situation?   **(1)**

The article goes on to discuss the advantages and disadvantages of learning a trade.

> **Wer einen Handwerksberuf erlernt hat und bereit ist zu arbeiten, der hat ganz bestimmt einen sicheren Arbeitsplatz und ist durchaus in der Lage, eine Familie zu ernähren. Und wer sich nicht scheut, wirklich hart zu arbeiten, der kann sogar sehr gut verdienen.**
>
> **In einigen Handwerkszweigen finden sich jedoch Nachteile, die man in Kauf nehmen muß. Hier kann man wohl drei Gruppen nennen: Einerseits die Handwerkszweige, bei denen man sich schmutzig macht, zum Beispiel die Bauberufe; dann die Bereiche mit Arbeitszeiten, die von den üblichen abweichen—nehmen Sie etwa den Bäcker oder auch den Metzger. Und schließlich die Leute, die samstags arbeiten müssen und so früh aufstehen müssen.**

(*d*) What advantages are there for someone who takes up a trade as a career? Write **three** things.   **(3)**

(*e*) Certain types of trade have difficulty in attracting young people. Why? Give **three** reasons.   **(3)**

4. Two girls, Natalie and Isabella, tell us about their hobbies and why they chose them.

Kreative Hobbies

Geige oder Klavier spielen sagen mir nichts. Saxophon ist viel außergewöhnlicher. Außerdem gibt's nicht viele, die das machen. Ich hab' mich in mein Sax' von Anfang an verliebt. Zwar braucht man viel Luft, aber ich bekam sofort einen Ton raus. Wenn ich Jazz oder Blues spiele, kann ich kreativ sein. Meine Eltern sind selber Künstler und verstehen mich voll, wenn ich verrückte Sachen machen will.

Natalie

(*a*) What appealed to Natalie about playing the saxophone? Write **three** things.

(3)

Menschen haben mich total fasziniert, daher habe ich so gern fotografiert. Man kann Menschen von einer Seite zeigen, die man sonst vielleicht nicht sieht. Daher habe ich in New York die Menschen fotografiert und eben nicht das Empire State Building.

Ich habe in der Schule einen Fotokurs mitgemacht, der echt was gebracht hat. Jetzt weiß ich einigermaßen über die Technik Bescheid. Als Folge hatte ich mehr Interesse an Schulfächern wie Chemie und Physik.

Isabella

(*b*) What attracted Isabella to photography? **(1)**

(*c*) How has her hobby influenced what she does in school? Write **two** things. **(2)**

[END OF QUESTION PAPER]

Total (31)

SCOTTISH
CERTIFICATE OF
EDUCATION
1996

TUESDAY, 28 MAY
3.10 PM – 3.40 PM
(APPROX)

GERMAN
STANDARD GRADE
Credit Level
Listening Transcript

Transcript—Credit Level

Instructions to reader(s):

For each item, read the English **once,** then read the German **twice**, with an interval of 7 seconds between the two readings. On completion of the second reading, pause for the length of time indicated in brackets after each item, to allow the candidates to write their answers.

Where special arrangements have been agreed in advance by the Board to allow the reading of the material, those sections marked **(f)** should be read by a female speaker and those marked **(m)** by a male: those sections marked **(t)** should be read by the teacher.

(t) You are spending two weeks of the summer holidays in Germany. You are staying in youth hostels.

Question number one.

One evening you arrive at the youth hostel in Berlin. Unfortunately the warden tells you it is full.

What does the warden suggest? Why does he suggest this?

(m) Es tut mir leid, aber ich habe von Ihnen keine Reservierung und wir haben keinen Platz mehr. Kommen Sie doch später einmal wieder! Manchmal kommen Leute nicht, und dann können Sie vielleicht doch noch ein Bett bekommen.

(40 seconds)

(t) Question number two.

A young German overhears your conversation with the warden and offers some advice.
What does she suggest you do? Write **two** things.

(f) Oh, das tut mir aber leid für dich. In Berlin ist so viel los, da mußt du schnell etwas finden. Es gibt einige billige Hotels in der Nähe vom Bahnhof. Und wenn du da nichts bekommst, dann geh zum Verkehrsamt. Dort wird man dir sicherlich helfen können.

(40 seconds)

(t) Question number three.

Eventually you find a room in a hall of residence at the university. While having a meal there that evening you get talking to two young Germans who are hitch-hiking round Germany. They talk about their experience of hitch-hiking.

Today has been a good day. What do they have to say about their experience of hitch-hiking in general? Write **three** things.

(f) **Heute hat es gut geklappt. Wir sind eine lange Strecke mit einem Lastwagen gefahren. Man weiß nämlich nie, wie weit man kommt. Manchmal verbringt man den ganzen Tag auf der Autobahn, ohne weiterzukommen. Aber manchmal lernt man auch nette Leute kennen, und einmal hat uns sogar eine Familie zum Essen eingeladen.**

(40 seconds)

(t) Question number four.

You have noticed that some cars in Germany travel extremely fast on the motorways. The two young people comment on this.

What does each of them say about the way people drive? Write **one** thing for each person.

(f) **—Es gibt auf vielen Strecken kein Tempolimit. Manche Leute fahren so schnell wie sie können.**

(m) **—Diese Leute denken nicht daran, daß viele Unfälle auf deutschen Autobahnen durch zu schnelles Fahren passieren. Sie bringen sich selbst und andere damit in Lebensgefahr.**

(40 seconds)

(t) Question number five.

One of the young people goes on to explain that attitudes to high speed driving are changing.

What signs are there of things changing? Write **two** things.

(f) **Manche Leute fahren jetzt langsamer, um die Umwelt zu schützen. Und der Druck auf die Regierung, ein Tempolimit einzuführen, wird deshalb immer stärker.**

(40 seconds)

(t) Question number six.

The following day you visit a suburb of East Berlin with your new friends. They explain how things are changing there.

What examples of changes are mentioned? Write **two** things.

m) **Diese alten Gebäude waren früher sehr schmutzig und in schlechtem Zustand. Sie werden jetzt überall restauriert. Es gibt jetzt auch viel mehr verschiedene Sachen in den Geschäften zu kaufen.**

(40 seconds)

(t) Question number seven.

You discuss where to have lunch. Your two friends can't agree on where you should go. Dieter prefers a fast food restaurant. Maren would prefer to go to a Turkish restaurant.

Why does Dieter prefer to go to a fast food restaurant? Write **two** things.

Why does Maren prefer a Turkish restaurant? Write **two** things.

(m) —Mensch! Das dauert immer so lange im Restaurant. Mit Selbstbedienung geht es viel schneller. Außerdem habe ich nicht mehr viel Geld.

(f) —Wir sind aber so viel gelaufen. Ich möchte mich jetzt ein bißchen hinsetzen. Hier in der Nähe ist ein türkisches Restaurant. Im Reiseführer steht, daß dieses Restaurant sehr gemütlich ist und es scheint auch gar nicht teuer zu sein. Es gibt dort ein Menü für 15 DM.

(*40 seconds*)

(t) Question number eight.

After lunch Dieter and Maren tell you about their plans for the next few days.

What do they plan to do in Marburg? Write **two** things.

(m) Wir wollen unsere Verwandten in Marburg besuchen. Die sehen wir so selten. Marburg ist nicht sehr weit von hier. Es ist so schön ruhig da und man kann sich ein paar Tage lang gut erholen. In letzter Zeit war bei uns so viel los.

(*40 seconds*)

(t) Question number nine.

Your two friends suggest you could see each other again.

Why do they suggest this? Write **two** things.

(f) Vielleicht könnten wir uns bald mal wieder treffen. Wir haben uns so gut mit dir verstanden. Wir kennen uns in vielen Städten Deutschlands gut aus. Wir würden dir gerne einiges zeigen.

(*40 seconds*)

(t) Question number ten.

Dieter and Maren suggest what you could do during the rest of your stay in Berlin.

What does Dieter suggest you do and why?

What does Maren suggest you do and why?

(m) —Du könntest eine Stadtführung zu Fuß mit allen Sehenswürdigkeiten machen. So lernt man am besten eine Stadt kennen. Und du kannst dir deine Zeit selber einteilen.

(f) —Fahr doch mal 'raus zu den Seen. In der Nähe von Berlin gibt es viele Seen. Dort sind nicht so viele Menschenmassen wie hier in der City. Es ist daher recht erholsam dort.

(*40 seconds*)

(t) End of test.

You now have 5 minutes to look over your answers.

[*END OF TRANSCRIPT*]

SCOTTISH
CERTIFICATE OF
EDUCATION
1996

TUESDAY, 28 MAY
3.10 PM – 3.40 PM
(APPROX)

GERMAN
STANDARD GRADE
Credit Level
Listening

Instructions to the Candidate

When you are told to do so, open your paper.

You will hear a number of short items in German. You will hear each item twice, then you will have time to write your answer.

Write your answers, **in English**, in the **separate** answer book provided.

You may take notes as you are listening to the German, but only in your answer book.

You may **not** use a German dictionary.

You are not allowed to leave the examination room until the end of the test.

Marks

You are spending two weeks of the summer holidays in Germany. You are staying in youth hostels.

1. One evening you arrive at the youth hostel in Berlin. Unfortunately the warden tells you it is full.

   (*a*) What does the warden suggest? **(1)**

   (*b*) Why does he suggest this? **(1)**

*   *   *   *   *

2. A young German overhears your conversation with the warden and offers some advice.

   What does she suggest you do? Write **two** things. **(2)**

*   *   *   *   *

3. Eventually you find a room in a hall of residence at the university. While having a meal there that evening you get talking to two young Germans who are hitch-hiking round Germany. They talk about their experience of hitch-hiking.

   Today has been a good day. What do they have to say about their experience of hitch-hiking in general? Write **three** things. **(3)**

*   *   *   *   *

4. You have noticed that some cars in Germany travel extremely fast on the motorways. The two young people comment on this.

   What does each of them say about the way people drive? Write **one** thing for each person. **(2)**

*   *   *   *   *

99

5. One of the young people goes on to explain that attitudes to high speed driving are changing.

What signs are there of things changing? Write **two** things. **(2)**

* * * * *

6. The following day you visit a suburb of East Berlin with your new friends. They explain how things are changing there.

What examples of changes are mentioned? Write **two** things. **(2)**

* * * * *

7. You discuss where to have lunch. Your two friends can't agree on where you should go.

Dieter prefers a fast food restaurant. Maren would prefer to go to a Turkish restaurant.

   (*a*) Why does Dieter prefer to go to a fast food restaurant? Write **two** things. **(2)**

   (*b*) Why does Maren prefer a Turkish restaurant? Write **two** things. **(2)**

* * * * *

8. After lunch Dieter and Maren tell you about their plans for the next few days.

What do they plan to do in Marburg? Write **two** things. **(2)**

* * * * *

9. Your two friends suggest you could see each other again.

Why do they suggest this? Write **two** things. **(2)**

* * * * *

10. Dieter and Maren suggest what you could do during the rest of your stay in Berlin.

   (*a*) What does Dieter suggest you do and why? **(2)**

   (*b*) What does Maren suggest you do and why? **(2)**

* * * * *

Total (25)

[END OF QUESTION PAPER]

SCOTTISH
CERTIFICATE OF
EDUCATION
1996

THURSDAY, 30 MAY
10.35 AM – 11.35 AM

GERMAN
STANDARD GRADE
Credit Level
(Optional Paper)
Writing

The following young people were asked how often they went shopping.

Ich gehe einmal in der Woche mit meiner Familie einkaufen. Ich mache das gern. Da kann ich mir Sachen aussuchen, die ich mag. Ich finde es nicht gut, daß meine Mutter allein einkaufen gehen muß. Deshalb helfe ich ihr.

Kristina, 16 Jahre

Ich gehe nie mit meiner Familie einkaufen. Es ist so langweilig und dauert so lange. Ich gehe lieber mit meinen Freunden einkaufen. Wir schauen uns die neuesten Sweat-Shirts an, gehen in unsere Lieblingsgeschäfte und kaufen auch mal Kassetten und CDs. Dann gehen wir noch zu McDonalds.

Michael, 15 Jahre

Ich gehe nur einmal im Monat einkaufen, weil ich sehr weit weg von der Stadt wohne. In meinem Dorf gibt es nur wenige Läden. Um etwas Auswahl zu haben, muß ich in eine Großstadt fahren.

Maria, 16 Jahre

Ich hasse es, einkaufen zu gehen. Ich gehe nie in Geschäfte. Ich finde es zu anstrengend und langweilig. Wenn ich irgendetwas kaufen muß, kaufe ich es aus Katalogen.

Peter, 15 Jahre

Now it's your turn!

Here are some questions you may wish to consider. You do not have to use all of them, and you are free to include other relevant ideas.

*   Do you go shopping often? Do you enjoy shopping, or do you find it boring? Do you prefer shopping alone, or with friends, or with your family?

*   What do you buy when you go shopping? You could write about one particular item you bought recently.

*   Are there good shops where you live? Do you have a favourite shop? Do you ever buy clothes or other items from mail order catalogues?

*   Do you think you get enough pocket money? Do you think some of your friends spend too much money?

Write about 200 words **in German**. You may use a German dictionary.

[*END OF QUESTION PAPER*]

SCOTTISH
CERTIFICATE OF
EDUCATION
1997

WEDNESDAY, 28 MAY
1.45 PM – 2.45 PM

GERMAN
STANDARD GRADE
Credit Level
Reading

Instructions to the Candidate

When you are told to do so, open your paper and write your answers **in English** in the **separate** answer book provided.

You may use a German dictionary.

Your German pen friend has sent you a magazine to read.   *Marks*

1. Alexander is a boy from Berlin who is physically disabled. He writes about some of the unpleasant things that sometimes happen to him on the way to school.

> **Ich fahre mit der U-Bahn zur Schule. Ich gehe den Weg zur U-Bahnstation meistens allein, weil meine Mitschüler so schnell laufen, daß ich nicht mithalten kann. Auf dem Bahnsteig steht eine Mutter mit ihrer kleinen Tochter. „Guck mal, Mami! Warum läuft der da so komisch?" fragt das Mädchen.**
>
> **Beim Aussteigen werde ich geschoben und gestoßen. „Nicht so langsam, andere wollen auch noch aussteigen", ruft jemand.**

(a) What unpleasant things happen to Alexander on the way to school? Write **three** things.   **(3)**

The last part of his journey is by bus. He describes an occasion when he sat on the seat reserved for disabled people.

> **Vom Bahnhof muß ich noch ein paar Stationen mit dem Bus fahren. Ich habe Glück und finde Platz auf der Bank vorne beim Fahrer, die für Behinderte reserviert ist. Eine ältere Frau steigt ein und kommt direkt auf meinen Platz zu. Sie sagt: „Geh mal weg da! Du siehst doch, daß ich mich setzen will."**
>
> **„Das ist ein Platz für Schwerbeschädigte", sagt mir eine zweite Frau. „Steh auf, und laß die Dame sitzen!"**
>
> **Dann sagt der Busfahrer: „So etwas Unverschämtes habe ich schon lange nicht mehr gesehen! Kannst du denn nicht lesen?" Nun habe ich aber genug. Ich halte meinen Ausweis hoch und rufe laut: „Das hier ist mein Behindertenausweis. Ich darf hier sitzen." Auf einmal wird es ganz still im Bus.**

(b) What did the following people say to him?

  (i)   the elderly woman

  (ii) the second woman

  (iii) the bus driver   **(3)**

(c) How did Alexander deal with the situation? Write **two** things.   **(2)**

2. This article is about the kind of role models young people have.

Hast du ein Vorbild?

Für viele junge Leute ist der Lieblingssportler ein Vorbild, für andere der Lieblingssänger.

Aber für uns alle waren unsere Eltern die ersten Vorbilder. Wie man läuft oder wie man spricht, das alles lernen wir von den Eltern!

Wenn wir größer werden, kommen andere Vorbilder an die Stelle der Eltern. Diese Vorbilder suchen wir uns nach Eigenschaften aus, die wir selbst gern hätten: Gutes Aussehen, Kraft, Erfolg, Geduld.

(*a*) Parents are our first role models. What do we learn from them? Write **two** things.

(2)

(*b*) How do we choose our role models when we are older?

(2)

Für einen Star oder ein Idol zu schwärmen ist nichts Schlimmes. Man muß sich nur klarmachen, daß auch berühmte Leute Fehler haben wie du und ich!

Aber Vorbilder müssen ja nicht immer Stars und reich sein. Es gibt auch Menschen, die Vorbilder sind—weil sie nicht an sich sondern an andere denken. Wie zum Beispiel die Leute, die in Afrika arbeiten und dort den armen Menschen helfen.

(*c*) What must we remember about the famous people we have as role models?

(1)

(*d*) Why might aid workers in Africa be good role models?

(1)

Marks

3. Three young people describe how they would try to get into conversation with someone they see in a café.

Franci

Es ist altmodisch, aber ich erwarte, daß die Jungen auf mich zugehen. Wenn mich jemand besonders interessiert, dann finde ich, man soll nicht einfach passiv da sitzen.

Ich stelle mich zum Beispiel im Café so hin, daß der Junge in meine Richtung gucken muß!

Das Wichtigste ist, daß der Junge mich anspricht und nicht umgekehrt.

Uwe

Wenn mir ein Mädchen im Café gefällt, dann setze ich mich einfach neben sie. Meistens überlege ich mir schon vorher, was ich sagen soll.

Zum Beispiel: „Ich weiß nicht, was ich bestellen soll, mach mir bitte einen Vorschlag." Viele lachen dann, und wir können weitersprechen!

Daniela

Ich versuche es erst mal mit Blickkontakt. In dem Moment, wo der Junge zufällig herschaut, gucke ich ihm in die Augen und dann sofort wieder weg. Dann versuche ich, mit ihm ins Gespräch zu kommen.

Franci, Uwe and Daniela all take different approaches when getting into conversation with someone.

(*a*) What approach does Franci take? Write **two** things. **(2)**

(*b*) What approach does Uwe take? Write **two** things. **(2)**

(*c*) What approach does Daniela take? Write **two** things. **(2)**

Marks

4. The writer of this article is a girl called Yvonne. She asks what would happen if pupils gave **teachers** grades, instead of the other way round.

- **Dann könnten die Kinder, wenn ein Lehrer etwas schlecht erklärt, sagen: „Das war ganz schlecht! Bis nächsten Montag bereiten Sie das besser vor!"**
- **. . . und die Kinder könnten zum Lehrer sagen: „Nehmen Sie sich ein Beispiel am Lehrer der Klasse 3d. Der ist ein guter Lehrer."**
- **. . . und dann hätten viele Lehrer vor der Schule genausoviel Angst wie viele Schüler.**

(*a*) What does Yvonne think would happen if pupils were to give teachers grades? Write **three** things. **(3)**

Viele Lehrer würden Hilfe brauchen, um bessere Lehrer zu werden. Und wer könnte einem Lehrer helfen? Natürlich ein Kind!

Und weil ich weiß, wie ein guter Lehrer sein sollte, könnte ich mir dann mit Nachhilfestunden mein Taschengeld aufbessern. Und bei dem, was wir in der Schule an Lehrern so haben, könnte ich auch noch meiner Mutter einen neuen Wintermantel kaufen.

(*b*) Yvonne thinks teachers would need help in order to become better teachers. Why does she feel qualified to help them improve? **(1)**

(*c*) How will she and her mother benefit? **(2)**

Total (26)

[END OF QUESTION PAPER]

SCOTTISH
CERTIFICATE OF
EDUCATION
1997

WEDNESDAY, 28 MAY
3.05 PM – 3.35 PM
(APPROX)

GERMAN
STANDARD GRADE
Credit Level
Listening Transcript

Transcript—Credit Level

Instructions to reader(s):

For each item, read the English **once,** then read the German **twice,** with an interval of 7 seconds between the two readings. On completion of the second reading, pause for the length of time indicated in brackets after each item, to allow the candidates to write their answers.

Where special arrangements have been agreed in advance to allow the reading of the material, those sections marked **(f)** should be read by a female speaker and those marked **(m)** by a male: those sections marked **(t)** should be read by the teacher.

(t) You are staying with your pen friend, Peter, in Germany.

Question number one.

One evening you are about to go to a party.

What advice does Peter's mother give you? Write **three** things.

(f)   **Wenn die Party erst nach Mitternacht zu Ende ist, lauf nicht allein nach Hause! Es ist zu gefährlich. Es ist schon viel passiert. Wenn ihr genug Leute findet, teilt euch ein Taxi! Oder übernachtet bei eurem Freund!**

(40 seconds)

(t) Question number two.

At the party, you are introduced to some of Peter's friends.

What questions do they ask you? Write **three** things.

(f) or (m)   **—Ich habe dich heute in der Schule gesehen, nicht wahr? Wie gefällt es dir in unserer Schule?**

(f) or (m)   **—Ist Deutsch deine erste Fremdsprache?**

(f) or (m)   **—Welche Sprache ist beliebter in Schottland—Deutsch oder Französisch?**

(40 seconds)

(t) Question number three.

One of Peter's friends is Ali, a boy from a Turkish family.

Why does Ali feel his family may one day go back to Turkey? Write **two** things.

(m)   **1965, als mein Vater nach Deutschland kam, gab es viele Arbeitsplätze. Junge Leute finden es heutzutage schwer, eine Stelle zu bekommen. Wenn ich keine Stelle oder keinen Studienplatz kriege, dann werden wir bestimmt in die Türkei zurückkehren. Und außerdem denke ich, daß meine Eltern Heimweh nach der Türkei haben und irgendwann zurückgehen wollen.**

(40 seconds)

(t) Question number four.

Ali tells you about how his father travelled to Germany when he first came from Turkey.

What does he say about the journey? Write **two** things.

(m)   **Die Familie meines Vaters wohnte auf dem Lande, und seine Reise hat mit einem Pferd angefangen. Vier Stunden mußte er reiten, bis zum Hauptbahnhof. Stellt euch das mal vor! Dann verbrachte er 36 Stunden im Zug.**

(40 seconds)

(t) Question number five.

Ali describes his father's first impressions of Germany.

What differences did he notice compared with his old life in Turkey? Write **two** things.

(m)   **Als er in Deutschland ankam, fand er das Leben völlig anders als in der Türkei. Die Leute hatten weniger Zeit—alles mußte immer sehr schnell gehen. Außerdem war er sehr einsam. Er vermißte seine Verwandten und Freunde.**

(40 seconds)

(t) Question number six.

Things slowly improved for Ali's father after his first two years in Germany.

In what ways did things improve? Write **two** things.

(m)   **Als die Familie nach zwei Jahren auch nach Deutschland kommen konnte, war er glücklicher, weil er wieder mit ihnen zusammen sein konnte. Und als wir Kinder, meine Geschwister und ich, in die Schule gingen, lernte er auch mehr Deutsche kennen.**

(40 seconds)

(t) Question number seven.

Two girls at the party, Susanne and Karoline, have different views about immigrants.

What does Susanne think immigrants could do to help themselves, and why?

(f)   **Ich habe nichts gegen Ausländer, aber sie sollten sich mehr anpassen. Kein Wunder, daß sie sich nicht integrieren können. Ihre Kultur und unsere Kultur passen nicht zusammen. Wenn sie freiwillig hierher kommen, müssen sie sich auch etwas bemühen.**

(40 seconds)

(t) Question number eight.

Karoline is more sympathetic towards immigrants.

What is her opinion? Write **two** things.

(f)   Aber viele Leute haben nur Angst vor dem Unbekannten. Ich finde, die Ausländer sollten ihre Kultur nicht aufgeben. Ich möchte jedenfalls keine türkischen, italienischen und griechischen Restaurants missen!

(40 seconds)

(t) Question number nine.

Later that evening, Peter tells you about an appointment he has with the doctor the following day.

What are the reasons for the appointment? Write **two** things.

(m)   Du, am Donnerstag habe ich einen Termin bei meinem Arzt. Im Winter habe ich einen Skiunfall gehabt und habe mir das rechte Bein gebrochen. Zweimal im Jahr muß er kontrollieren, daß alles noch in Ordnung ist.

(40 seconds)

(t) Question number ten.

Peter suggests what you could do while he is at the doctor's.

What does he suggest? Write **two** things.

(m)   Während ich da bin, könntest du vielleicht den Dom besuchen und auf den Turm klettern. Von dort oben hat man einen wunderschönen Blick über die ganze Stadt.

(40 seconds)

(t) Question number eleven.

Peter suggests what you could do together after that.

What does he suggest? Write **three** things.

(m)   Zu Mittag können wir in einem Schnellimbiß essen gehen und dann eventuell auf dem See Kanu fahren. Und ich habe von einem Freund gehört, daß es im Stadtmuseum gerade eine Ausstellung übers Kino gibt. Sie läuft noch bis nächste Woche. Wenn du Lust hast, können wir auch dahin gehen.

(40 seconds)

(t) End of test.

You now have 5 minutes to look over your answers.

[END OF TRANSCRIPT]

SCOTTISH
CERTIFICATE OF
EDUCATION
1997

WEDNESDAY, 28 MAY
3.05 PM – 3.35 PM
(APPROX)

GERMAN
STANDARD GRADE
Credit Level
Listening

Instructions to the Candidate

When you are told to do so, open your paper.

You will hear a number of short items in German. You will hear each item twice, then you will have time to write your answer.

Write your answers, **in English**, in the **separate** answer book provided.

You may take notes as you are listening to the German, but only in your answer book.

You may **not** use a German dictionary.

You are not allowed to leave the examination room until the end of the test.

Marks

You are staying with your pen friend, Peter, in Germany.

1. One evening you are about to go to a party.
    What advice does Peter's mother give you? Write **three** things.   (3)

*   *   *   *   *

2. At the party, you are introduced to some of Peter's friends.
    What questions do they ask you? Write **three** things.   (3)

*   *   *   *   *

3. One of Peter's friends is Ali, a boy from a Turkish family.
    Why does Ali feel his family may one day go back to Turkey? Write **two**
    things.   (2)

*   *   *   *   *

4. Ali tells you about how his father travelled to Germany when he first came
    from Turkey.
    What does he say about the journey? Write **two** things.   (2)

*   *   *   *   *

Marks

5. Ali describes his father's first impressions of Germany.

   What differences did he notice compared with his old life in Turkey? Write **two** things.

   (2)

   *   *   *   *   *

6. Things slowly improved for Ali's father after his first two years in Germany.

   In what ways did things improve? Write **two** things.

   (2)

   *   *   *   *   *

7. Two girls at the party, Susanne and Karoline, have different views about immigrants.

   What does Susanne think immigrants could do to help themselves, and why?

   (2)

   *   *   *   *   *

8. Karoline is more sympathetic towards immigrants.

   What is her opinion? Write **two** things.

   (2)

   *   *   *   *   *

9. Later that evening, Peter tells you about an appointment he has with the doctor the following day.

   What are the reasons for the appointment? Write **two** things.

   (2)

   *   *   *   *   *

10. Peter suggests what you could do while he is at the doctor's.

    What does he suggest? Write **two** things.

    (2)

    *   *   *   *   *

11. Peter suggests what you could do together after that.

    What does he suggest? Write **three** things.

    (3)

    *   *   *   *   *

Total (25)

[END OF QUESTION PAPER]

SCOTTISH
CERTIFICATE OF
EDUCATION
1997

FRIDAY, 30 MAY
10.35 AM – 11.35 AM

GERMAN
STANDARD GRADE
Credit Level
(Optional Paper)
Writing

These young people were asked to write about their life at school and their plans for the future.

Stefan

Schule finde ich furchtbar. Wir haben immer so viele Hausaufgaben. Ich helfe viel lieber meinem Vater auf dem Bauernhof. Ich möchte auch später Landwirt werden wie mein Vater. Ich glaube, ich gehe in der zehnten Klasse ab.

Claudia

Ich gehe gern zur Schule. Meine Lieblingsfächer sind Französisch und Deutsch. Nach meinem Abitur möchte ich für ein Jahr nach Frankreich gehen und dort arbeiten. Ich möchte meine Sprachkenntnisse verbessern, weil ich gern Fremdsprachensekretärin werden will.

Markus

Mein Lieblingsfach in der Schule ist Musik. Ich spiele Flöte. Während meines Arbeitspraktikums habe ich in einem Musikgeschäft gearbeitet. Ich denke, ich werde später auch ein Geschäft haben und Flöten bauen.

Anna

Ich gehe nicht so gerne in die Schule, aber ich mache gern Sport und Kunst. In Kunst habe ich einen sehr netten Lehrer, der den Unterricht sehr interessant macht. Ich habe vor, die Schule vor dem Abitur zu verlassen, weil ich eine Lehre als Tischler machen möchte. Dafür braucht man kein Abitur.

What are your thoughts on your life at school?

Here are some ideas you may wish to consider. You do not have to use all of them, and you are free to include other relevant ideas.

* What subjects do you like at school?
* What don't you like so much about school?
* How do you get on with your teachers?
* Have you done any work experience?
* Have you any plans for further study?
* What sort of job would you like to do eventually?

Write about 200 words **in German**. You may use a German dictionary.

[END OF QUESTION PAPER]

SCOTTISH
CERTIFICATE OF
EDUCATION
1998

TUESDAY, 26 MAY
10.15 AM – 11.15 AM

GERMAN
STANDARD GRADE
Credit Level
Reading

Instructions to the Candidate

When you are told to do so, open your paper and write your answers **in English** in the **separate** answer book provided.

You may use a German dictionary.

Your pen friend has sent you a German magazine to read.   *Marks*

1. Three young Germans write about their experiences at English Language summer schools.

Wie war's?
Did you like
it?

"Ich war in Elgin.   Japaner, Franzosen, Spanier—auf der Sommerschule in Elgin (Morayshire) in Schottland waren viele Nationen vertreten. Wir hatten jeden Tag zwei Stunden Schule und konnten danach Sportarten wie Kanufahren oder Fechten ausprobieren. Ungewohnt waren für mich die strengen Regeln: Die Mädchen durften sich zum Beispiel nicht mit Jungen treffen.   Natürlich sind wir trotzdem nachts aus dem Fenster geklettert und haben zusammen Partys gefeiert."

Birgit

(*a*)   How was the day at Birgit's summer school divided up?   **(1)**

(*b*)   Which school rule did she find surprising?   **(1)**

(*c*)   How did the young people overcome this problem?   **(1)**

Marks

„Ich war in Torquay. Torquay ist ein ganz kleiner englischer Küstenort, der jedes Jahr von Sprachgruppen überschwemmt wird. Die Einheimischen schienen von uns Sprachschülern etwas genervt, so daß es schwer war, mit Gleichaltrigen in Kontakt zu kommen. Aber meine nette Gastfamilie behandelte mich wie ihren eigenen Sohn. Wir haben viel gemeinsam unternommen."

(*d*)   What did Sven find difficult about his time in Torquay?   **(1)**

(*e*)   What did he enjoy about his visit?   **(1)**

„Ich war in Chicago. Meinen Amerika-Aufenthalt hatte ich mir etwas anders vorgestellt. Meine erste Gastfamilie in Chicago war ein echter Schocker. In der Wohnung sah es aus, als hätte eine Bombe eingeschlagen. Dazu mußte ich mit den zwei kleinen Kindern ein Zimmer teilen. Zum Glück konnte ich nach einer Woche in eine andere Familie wechseln. Der Sprachunterricht zusammen mit Schülern aus aller Welt machte wirklich Spaß."

(*f*)   Why were things difficult at first for Christoph? (Write **two** things.)   **(2)**

(*g*)   What did he particularly like about the course?   **(1)**

Marks

2. This article is about a woman who does what was once considered a man's job and a man who does what used to be considered a woman's job.

Wenn Stephanie Kuhn als Kind mit ihrer Mutter an einem Bahnübergang stand und eine Diesellokomotive vorbeibrauste, dann sagte sie, „So eine möchte ich auch mal fahren!" Später wurde sie Lokomotivführerin.

Wer eine moderne Diesellokomotive fahren will, muß sich gut konzentrieren können. Stephanie muß natürlich die Fahrpläne genau wissen. Sie darf nicht zu schnell und nicht zu langsam fahren, muß die Signale beachten. Als Lokomotivführerin trägt sie die volle Verantwortung.

„Ich mag die Arbeit sehr, aber der Schichtdienst macht manchmal Probleme. Mein Mann ist ebenfalls Lokomotivführer, und wir müssen also unsere Arbeitszeiten abstimmen, damit einer von uns jeden Abend zu Hause ist und für die Kinder sorgt."

(*a*) What first made Stephanie decide to become an engine driver? **(1)**

(*b*) What is required to be a good engine driver? Write **three** things. **(3)**

(*c*) How does she get round the problem of coping with her children and doing shift work?

(1)

typisch Mann?

Jens Unger is a male midwife. (A midwife is a nurse who specialises in the delivery of babies.)

Jens Unger

→

Entbindungs-pfleger

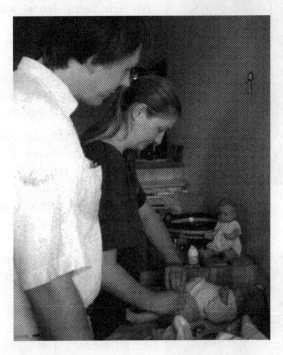

„Für diesen Beruf habe ich mich erst vor wenigen Jahren entschieden", erzählt Jens. „Damals habe ich im Krankenhaus gearbeitet und durfte bei einer Geburt dabei sein. Die Geburt dauerte viele Stunden. Es war sehr schön, zu sehen, wie glücklich und dankbar die Frau war, als ihr Kind endlich da war! Darum wollte ich Entbindungspfleger werden."

Als Entbindungspfleger muß Jens jede Menge über Medizin wissen. „Meine Aufgabe ist es aber auch, die Blicke und Bewegungen der schwangeren Frau richtig zu verstehen. Ich muß auch erkennen, wann es für die Frau und das Baby gefährlich wird."

(*d*) What made Jens decide he wanted to become a midwife? (Write **two** things.) **(2)**

(*e*) What is required to be a good midwife? (Write **three** things.) **(3)**

1998

3. Two young people tell us what the word "**beauty**" means to them. Each of them had experiences when they were young which affected how they later thought about the subject of beauty.

Was heißt hier „schön"?

Thomas, 17

Wie jemand aussieht, ist für mich nicht so wichtig. Das beeindruckt mich gar nicht.

Als ich zehn Jahre war, habe ich mir das Gesicht schwer verbrannt. In vier Operationen wurde mir mein Gesicht einigermaßen wiederhergestellt. Am Anfang war es schwer, denn ich wurde oft auf der Straße angestarrt, besonders von jungen Leuten. Später jedoch habe ich es ignoriert, und ich bin dadurch selbstbewußter geworden.

Ich habe gelernt, das Äußere nicht mehr so wichtig zu nehmen, und meine Einstellung zu „was ist schön?" hat sich dadurch geändert. Was für mich jetzt wichtig ist, sind die Charaktereigenschaften: „Schön" ist, wenn jemand gut mit anderen Leuten umgehen kann und Toleranz zeigt.

Anja, 16

Das typische Schönheitsideal hat mich eine Zeitlang kaputtgemacht. Mit zehn Jahren war ich dick, trug eine Brille und wurde von meinen Klassenkameraden ständig ausgelacht. In den Zeitschriften sah ich die dünnen Models und ich habe mir eingeredet: so mußt du aussehen! Ich habe alles getan, um abzunehmen. Keinen Zucker mehr essen und Sport treiben. Ich habe so viel abgenommen, daß ich krank geworden bin. Ich lag wochenlang im Krankenhaus und habe ein Schuljahr wiederholen müssen.

Heute fühle ich mich wohl, so wie ich bin, und mache mir keine Gedanken mehr ums Aussehen. „Schön" bedeutet für mich deshalb, das Leben positiv zu betrachten und innerlich zufrieden zu sein.

(a) What were the experiences which affected how they later thought about beauty? Write **two** things for each person. **(4)**

(b) What does "beauty" mean for them now? Write **two** things for each person. **(4)**

Total (26)

[END OF QUESTION PAPER]

SCOTTISH
CERTIFICATE OF
EDUCATION
1998

TUESDAY, 26 MAY
1.00 PM – 1.30 PM
(APPROX)

GERMAN
STANDARD GRADE
Credit Level
Listening Transcript

Transcript—Credit Level

> **Instructions to reader(s):**
>
> For each item, read the English **once**, then read the German **twice**, with an interval of 7 seconds between the two readings. On completion of the second reading, pause for the length of time indicated in brackets after each item, to allow the candidates to write their answers.
>
> Where special arrangements have been agreed in advance to allow the reading of the material, those sections marked **(f)** should be read by a female speaker and those marked **(m)** by a male: those sections marked **(t)** should be read by the teacher.

(t) During the summer you spend two weeks at an international summer school for young people in Munich.

(f) or (m)   **Während des Sommers besuchst du zwei Wochen lang eine internationale Sommerschule für Jugendliche in München.**

(t) Question number one.

When you arrive, you meet two fellow students.

How did they travel to the summer school? Write **two** things.

(f) or (m)   **Hallo! Wir sind gerade angekommen. Wir sind beide aus Finnland und haben uns auf der Fähre getroffen. Die Überfahrt haben wir am Freitag gemacht, und dann sind wir gemeinsam mit dem Zug von Kiel hierhergereist. Woher kommst du?**

(40 seconds)

(t) Question number two.

You all go to the reception desk, where you are given some information.

What information are you given? Write **three** things.

(f) or (m)   **Ihr habt euch schon eingetragen? Ja? Gut. Also, ihr drei seid im Zimmer 24. Das liegt im zweiten Stock. Schlafsäcke und Handtücher findet ihr auf den Betten. Ich wünsche euch allen viel Spaß.**

(40 seconds)

(t) Question number three.

You are told to come to the hall at 11.00 am. The group leader tells you about arrangements for meals and snacks.

What does she tell you? Write **three** things.

(f)   **Es gibt drei Mahlzeiten pro Tag. Die Zeiten findet ihr am Brett vor dem Speisesaal. Vegetarier sollten sich heute bei der Küche melden. Am Kiosk kann man außerdem noch Süßigkeiten und Getränke kaufen.**

(40 seconds)

(t) Question number four.

The group leader also tells you about the programme for the afternoon.

What must you do this afternoon? Write **two** things.

(f)   **Heute Nachmittag treffen wir uns alle um 2.00 Uhr im Gemeinschaftsraum. Jeder soll sich kurz vorstellen, Name, Wohnort, usw. und ein wenig über sein Heimatland erzählen. Und das soll natürlich auf Deutsch sein!**

(40 seconds)

(t) Question number five.

During the week you will be working in pairs. The leader sets you a task for the following day.

What is the task? Write **two** things.

(f)   **Ihr beide werdet zusammen arbeiten. Morgen geht ihr auf die Straße. Ihr macht eine Umfrage. Ihr sollt zwanzig verschiedene Leute fragen, was sie für die Umwelt tun.**

(40 seconds)

(t) Question number six.

You make plans for the free time you have in the early evening.

What do your friends suggest? Write **two** things.

(f) or
(m)   **Wir haben heute so lange herumgesessen. Wir müssen unbedingt an die frische Luft. Unterwegs vom Bahnhof habe ich nicht weit von hier ein schönes Freibad gesehen. Wie wär's, wenn wir dahin gehen? Danach können wir uns vielleicht noch dieses Stadtviertel ansehen.**

(40 seconds)

(t) Question number seven.

At the meal, Matti, one of your friends, tells you why he is at the summer school.

Why is Matti here? Write **two** things.

(m)   **Ich bin hier, um mein Deutsch zu verbessern. Ich suche zur Zeit eine Stelle als Verkäufer bei einer Exportfirma in Helsinki. Sprachkenntnisse sind für solche Stellen besonders wichtig.**

(40 seconds)

(t) Question number eight.

Also at your table is Janna, a girl from Prague in the Czech Republic. She tells you about the course she was on last summer.

Why did she enjoy the course? Write **two** things.

(f)   **Letztes Jahr habe ich an einem Sommerkurs in Frankreich teilgenommen. Das war toll. Ich habe junge Leute aus ganz Europa kennengelernt. Am Ende waren wir alle feste Freunde und wir schreiben uns immer noch.**

(40 seconds)

(t) Question number nine.

Matti asks Janna about Prague.

What does he ask Janna?

(m)   **Ich war vor vier Jahren als Schüler in Prag. Was hat sich dort in der Zwischenzeit geändert?**

(40 seconds)

(t) Question number ten.

Janna talks about the changes that have taken place in Prague.

What does she say? Write **three** things.

(f)   **Es kommen jetzt viel mehr Touristen als früher aus Westeuropa und auch aus den USA. Die Stadt verdient ganz schön viel daran, aber die Straßen in der Stadtmitte sind jetzt leider immer voll von Autos und Reisebussen.**

(40 seconds)

(t) Question number eleven.

After the evening meal, one of the Finnish boys, Järmo, decides he does not want to go out.

What is he complaining about? Write **two** things.

(m)   **Ich glaube, ich bleibe heute Abend lieber hier im Haus. Nach meiner langen Reise fühle ich mich total fertig. Mein ganzer Körper tut mir weh. Ich lege mich ins Bett, dann bin ich morgen hoffentlich wieder fit.**

(40 seconds)

(t) Question number twelve.

Matti has a good idea.

What does he suggest to Järmo?

(m)   **Hör mal, Järmo. Wir gehen direkt zum Freibad. Wir bleiben höchstens eine Stunde im Wasser. Dann setzen wir uns ins Café am Eingang. Wenn du dich besser fühlst, kannst du uns dort treffen.**

(40 seconds)

(t) End of test.

You now have 5 minutes to look over your answers.

[END OF TRANSCRIPT]

SCOTTISH
CERTIFICATE OF
EDUCATION
1998

TUESDAY, 26 MAY
1.00 PM – 1.30 PM
(APPROX)

GERMAN
STANDARD GRADE
Credit Level
Listening

Instructions to the Candidate

When you are told to do so, open your paper.

You will hear a number of short items in German. You will hear each item twice, then you will have time to write your answer.

Write your answers, **in English**, in the **separate** answer book provided.

You may take notes as you are listening to the German, but only in your answer book.

You may **not** use a German dictionary.

You are not allowed to leave the examination room until the end of the test.

Marks

During the summer you spend two weeks at an international summer school for young people in Munich.

Während des Sommers besuchst du zwei Wochen lang eine internationale Sommerschule für Jugendliche in München.

1. When you arrive, you meet two fellow students.

    How did they travel to the summer school? Write **two** things. **(2)**

    *   *   *   *   *

2. You all go to the reception desk, where you are given some information.

    What information are you given? Write **three** things. **(3)**

    *   *   *   *   *

3. You are told to come to the hall at 11.00 am. The group leader tells you about arrangements for meals and snacks.

    What does she tell you? Write **three** things. **(3)**

    *   *   *   *   *

4. The group leader also tells you about the programme for the afternoon.

    What must you do this afternoon? Write **two** things. **(2)**

    *   *   *   *   *

5. During the week you will be working in pairs. The leader sets you a task for the following day.

    What is the task? Write **two** things. **(2)**

    *   *   *   *   *

6. You make plans for the free time you have in the early evening.

    What do your friends suggest? Write **two** things. **(2)**

    *   *   *   *   *

7. At the meal, Matti, one of your friends, tells you why he is at the summer school.

    Why is Matti here? Write **two** things. **(2)**

    *   *   *   *   *

Marks

8. Also at your table is Janna, a girl from Prague in the Czech Republic. She tells you about the course she was on last summer.

   Why did she enjoy the course? Write **two** things. (2)

* * * * *

9. Matti asks Janna about Prague.
   What does he ask Janna? (1)

* * * * *

10. Janna talks about the changes that have taken place in Prague.
    What does she say? Write **three** things. (3)

* * * * *

11. After the evening meal, one of the Finnish boys, Järmo, decides he does not want to go out.
    What is he complaining about? Write **two** things. (2)

* * * * *

12. Matti has a good idea. What does he suggest to Järmo? (1)

* * * * *

Total (25)

[*END OF QUESTION PAPER*]

SCOTTISH
CERTIFICATE OF
EDUCATION
1998

TUESDAY, 26 MAY
2.50 PM – 3.50 PM

GERMAN
STANDARD GRADE
Credit Level
(Optional Paper)
Writing

The following young people were asked about their summer holiday plans.

Im Juni fahre ich nach Dänemark. Ich verbringe zwei Wochen dort. Ich habe vor, in Jugendherbergen zu übernachten. Ohne Eltern! Das wird echt super sein.

Konrad, 16 Jahre

Dieses Jahr fliege ich zum ersten Mal mit meinen Eltern in die Türkei. Es soll unheimlich warm sein und ich hoffe, den ganzen Tag am Strand zu faulenzen. Leider wird mein Vater Volleyball und Tennis spielen, und meine Mutti wird bestimmt wandern gehen. Sport und Wandern mag ich nicht.

Ramona, 15 Jahre

Im August fahre ich mit meinen Freunden an die Nordsee. Dort verbringen wir fünf Tage. Wir fahren jedes Jahr an denselben Ort und treffen Freunde von vorigen Jahren. Mit meinen Freunden verstehe ich mich gut. Das ist für mich der ideale Urlaub.

Jens, 17 Jahre

Dieses Jahr bleibe ich daheim. Ich möchte aber Tagesausflüge machen, denn es gibt viele schöne Städte und Dörfer in der Umgebung. Zu Hause kann man sich auch gut erholen.

Hannelore, 16 Jahre

Now it's your turn!

Here are some questions you may wish to consider. You do not have to use all of them, and you are free to include other relevant ideas.

* Where do you usually go on holiday?
* What do you plan to do this year?
* Are you going away or staying at home?
* How will you spend the time?
* With whom?
* Where?

Write about 200 words **in German**. You may use a German dictionary.

[END OF QUESTION PAPER]

NOTES

Printed by Bell & Bain Ltd., Glasgow, Scotland.